LAST WORDS

Don Paterson was born in Dundee in 1963. He works as a musician and editor. His poetry collections are *Nil Nil* (1993), *God's Gift to Women* (1997) and *The Eyes* (1999), and he has edited *101 Sonnets – From Shakespeare to Heaney*. He has been the recipient of several literary awards, including the T. S. Eliot Prize and the Geoffrey Faber Memorial Prize. He currently lives in Edinburgh.

Jo Shapcott is the author of three award-winning books of poetry: *Electroplating the Baby* (1988), *Phrase Book* (1992) and *My Life Asleep* (1998). A compendium of her poems, *Her Book*, will be published in 2000. She is co-editor of an anthology of contemporary poetry: *Emergency Kit: Poems for Strange Times* (1996) and her work can be found in *Penguin Modern Poets 12*.

LAST WORDS

New Poetry for the New Century

EDITED BY DON PATERSON AND JO SHAPCOTT

PICADOR

First published 1999 by Picador
an imprint of Macmillan Publishers Ltd
25 Eccleston Place, London SW1W 9NF
Basingstoke and Oxford
Associated companies throughout the world
www.macmillan.co.uk

In association with The Salisbury Festival

ISBN 0 330 39047 3

1 3 5 7 9 8 6 4 2

A CIP catalogue record for this book is available from
the British Library.

Typeset by SetSystems Ltd, Saffron Walden, Essex
Printed and bound in Great Britain by
Mackays of Chatham plc, Chatham, Kent

Contents

Introduction

Despite its title – which, once suggested, stuck to the project like a limpet – the Salisbury Last Words festival was not conceived by its director, Helen Marriage, solely as millennial farewell. Her idea was to stake out a new territory by offering alternative ways that poetry might present its face to the public in the future. Having done so, she asked us to colonize it with the work of many of the poets who would matter in the coming century. So it was that around ninety of our best poets were commissioned by the Salisbury Festival to write new poems that would find a home not only in this anthology, but also somewhere in the city, where they would be on display during the last week of October 1999.

The first objective was that, throughout, this festival should engage people in the physical act of reading poetry. Reading a poem demands a different, more active participation on the part of the reader than does hearing it read: the little journey of the poem – whether easy or difficult, long or short, dark or daylit – has to be made alone, and in the process the poem becomes the reader's own.

The second was to try to restore some of the faith lost in the word as a human spell, and in the poem as a kind of sympathetic magic. No one could have dreamt up a better situation for the project: the spire of Salisbury Cathedral rises above it like a great lightning rod or radio mast, both conductor and broadcaster. It was our hope, in physically centring much of the work around the cathedral, to focus attention on the spiritual dimension present in much of the work – a dimension that many potential readers of contemporary poetry mistakenly believe to be absent from it.

While this was the broader gesture, it was never our intention that the work itself should have to embrace either of these spiritual or millennial themes: the manner of their presentation would take care of that. We did all we could to encourage the participating poets to be limited only by the formal demands of their specific commission – and the result was work of kaleidoscopic variety, truly 'the drunkenness of things being various'.

When the poems started pouring in at the start of April, our excitement was hard to contain: here were 'civic' poems in the best possible sense – different, perhaps, from the poets' usual output, less in their substance than in the form of their address; this had everywhere an openness and a generosity about it that lent the whole project a real uniformity of spirit.

This may have had something to do with the fact that, for once, we could offer the poets a guarantee that their poems would be *read*. All most poets want is a community that finds them useful. Communities badly want to find a use not for them, but for poetry: this, we believe, has been the source of much recent confusion on the matter of how poets should be employed.

Poets should more often be put to work doing what they do best – writing poems. Not just giving readings, or running workshops, although it's true that the simple presence of poets in the community can spark enthusiasm for words, for both reading and writing. But just as a city's buildings should be designed by architects, so its poems should be written by its poets. Poetry is just another way the community expresses itself, and a community needs poets (as it has always done) to find an articulate voice for its sorrows and joys; to encapsulate its lives and histories that they might be properly commemorated, and so committed to memory; to find an expressive form for its spiritual aspirations; to offer it visions of a moral and aesthetic realm it would prefer to inhabit; to offer it the wit and humour and the insight by which it makes life toler able, and the imagination to make everything new and strange again. *Last Words*, in one sense, was an attempt to reunite that community with its poetry, not its poets, and explore the ways in which this might be effected in the future.

The festival tried to achieve this by making poems physically impossible to avoid. There were poems carved into stone and placed in the grounds and cloisters of Salisbury Cathedral. Two stained-glass windows were also donated to the cathedral. A special service – a 'poetry liturgy' – was held in the cathedral too. A giant poem unfolded throughout the week on scaffolding outside. Poems were flown above the town from light aircraft. Poems were grown into fields and lit up in fireworks. There was a comedy night when poems were improvised at suggestions from the audi- ence. Poem-films were shown at the cinema. Poems were displayed in shop windows. Poems were tattooed permanently on to skin and hennaed on to bodies.

Poems appeared on beer mats, billboards, bus tickets, carrier bags and tray liners. At night, poems were projected on to Salisbury's public buildings. Poems were hung in the Arts Centre as if they were paintings. Poems were illustrated by giant origami displays. Poems were tiled in public toilets. Poets were placed 'in residence' for the week on the local radio station and the *Salisbury Journal* news desk, in the army barracks, the police station and the cathedral itself. Poems were franked on to letters. Competitions to write the best circle-shaped poem were held in schools, while a 'worst haiku' competition was run in the pubs. Anti-poetry demonstrations were staged in the town. A candlelit poetry 'reading' was held in the cathedral, with the poems read in silence, each inward reading punctuated by music specially commissioned for the occasion.

The idea was to have no live readings whatsoever, and to see if a week-long event could be sustained in a purely text-based way – in other words, by turning the town into a giant book. People would simply come across poems wherever they went. Poetry's notorious 'difficulty' is often more a matter of its presentation and misrepresentation than anything intrinsic to the medium itself. This, we hoped, would clear the road towards it, and allow readers to come across the poem the way they would a piece of municipal sculpture – to wonder or jeer or laugh or sigh at, but always to engage with.

Above all, these casual, serendipitous readers would have poems all around them which they could read – or not – in their own time. None of this, however, is to deny that the live reading of a poem – a poem's particular way of making the air vibrate – is any less its final form than its page-life. Put this fact together with a reader of great power and presence, and a full house, and you can have a pretty unforgettable experience. But poetry might amost be defined as the art of rereading: all true poems have a valuable secret freight which it takes time to discover and unpack. *Last Words* simply attempts to redress the balance, to give the poem back to the reader.

This notion proved universally popular among the poets we commissioned. Poets quite often want nothing more than to have their poems grow up and leave home and make their own way in the world, not to be read as a form of autobiography, or something they must continually answer for and defend in public.

We'd like to pay tribute to the Salisbury Festival itself and, in particular, to its director Helen Marriage; *Last Words* was her idea, and it was her committment and vision that saw it become a reality. We'd also like to thank her dedicated staff, especially Cecilia Evans. Thanks are also due to the many funders and other partners in the project: the Arts Council of England, the Dean and Chapter of Salisbury Cathedral, the *Salisbury Journal*, Spire Radio, the police and army in Salisbury, Salisbury Arts Centre, PahBoom Fireworks, the many individual local writers and writers' groups who lent their support, as well as the many others who offered their contribution after this book went to press – and, above all, to the citizens of Salisbury who paused to read the book into which their city had been transformed.

Our last words must be reserved for the poets whose work is collected here, and who responded so generously to what one poet described as their 'strange and beautiful' commissions. If the reader finds serious omissions here, we would hope that they came about because the poets approached – for one reason or another – were unable to take on the commission. We are not apologists for this anthology: while we may have suggested the list of poets, we didn't choose the poems, and have our own favourites. The poets are here representing only themselves: at least this guarantees the book a democracy of taste.

So welcome to the little city of *Last Words*; by no means an ideal one – contrary, squabbling, various – but united around the flag of the word, the belief that it can make a difference. That is its polity and its creed. We hope it's a place where you'll want to spend more of your time.

Don Paterson and Jo Shapcott

DANNIE ABSE

Gaiety at the Crematorium

Later, when Itzig read Heidegger,
absurdly wide-awake, he took out
his life-savings from the Halifax,
arranged a mock funeral for nobody.

Then, in the rear, carrying a banner
DREAD REVEALS NOTHING
he followed the hired procession
into the crematorium.

No priest, mawkish, puffed a eulogy
since nobody lay in that coffin.
The old-timers, the once hip jazz men,
encored the old Duke Ellington tunes
as the coffin on the conveyor,
in slow motion, slid out of sight.
Their knock-out gig concluded with
'Don't get around much any more.'

Then the decorous Treorchy Male Choir
euphoniously sang 'Smoke Gets in Your Eyes'
and the feet-tapping congregation
suitably dressed in serious toggery,
pronounced it all to be the best ever
ceremony at the crematorium.

Everybody, sober, had a grand time
except the ghostly-looking mortician
who felt that burning an empty coffin
– a first class polished oak one at that –
was a ghastly sinful waste.

FLEUR ADCOCK

A Visiting Angel

My angel's wearing dressing-up clothes –
her sister's ballet-skirt, her mother's top,
some spangles, a radiant smile.

She looks as if she might take off
and float in the air – whee! But of course
you've guessed: she's not an angel really.

Her screeches when you try to dress her
make the neighbours think of child abuse.
She has to be in the mood for clothes.

Once, for the sake of peace, when she wouldn't even
part with her soggy night-time nappy,
I took her to the shops in her pyjamas.

And what about the shoe she left on the train?
But then she sat like Cinderella,
serene and gracious, trying on the new ones.

Has she been spoilt? Her big sister,
no less pretty, gave up the cuteness contest
and settled for being the sensible one.

It's tough being sister to an angel
(a burden I bore for years myself),
but being an angel's grandmother is bliss.

I want to buy her French designer outfits.
Madness. It would be cheaper and more fun
to go to Paris. So we all do that.

A special deal on Eurostar.
Halfway there, she comes to sit beside me
on Daddy's knee, and stares into my face.

'Fleur', she says thoughtfully, 'I love you.'
Wow! That's angel-talk, no doubt of it.
Where can I buy her a halo and some wings?

FRED D'AGUIAR

Foot Print

If cartilage, muscle, nail and gristle
fills a shot-glass, and the little
that's a lot pours tidily into a pouch
no bigger than a sparrow's throat,
then your foot, delicate as a thistle,
eight months old and frost-brittle,
occupies exactly this open mouth
leather shoe, light enough to float.

Son, mould yourself to your first pair
for the heady climb from knees and hands.
Once up and running, what you wear,
not your soles, scorches in hot sands,
wards off corns, bunions, claw toes:
shoes fit for feet, feet fit for shoes.

SIMON ARMITAGE

The Way

It's a short walk from the house of a friend,
the Way, and leads only from here to there,
from its starting point to its very end.

It forms a switchback two spans wide at most.
Its length is possibly measured in strides,
though far too long to bother to keep count,

or measured in minutes – the time it takes
to travel the Way at an even pace.
It begins as a style, ends as a gate.

Going out, to the right side of the Way,
is a fence overcome by undergrowth,
and below the banking a railway line,

and freight trains have been known to shuttle through,
causing animal life to freeze or move,
plant life to juggle or cling to its fruit.

Overdue blackberries, heavy with blood.
Some bird under cover of grass, half choked,
coughs up the sound of the frog in its throat.

To the left side of the Way, going out,
is a field of barley, standing its ground.
So on the home leg, these things turn around.

What great garden the Way would be, green lane
rolled out from a doorstep in a straight line.
What great lawn, and a long by narrow job

with a motorized blade to keep it as cropped
as this. A tractor, dragging a cutter,
would see to the work in a single pass,

but there are no tracks. No footprints either,
as if each step took back the mark it made.
We are all as different as we are the same.

The Way at first light or just before dusk,
deserted of course, except for yourself
of course, and a black dog ranging forward

and back, bringing sticks and stones in its mouth
like memories of the future, premonitions
of the past. De-cap this morning's mushroom

with the toe-end of a boot, or don't;
tonight, take home a token of the place –
pick out a plant that answers to its name.

The Way, like so, where its opposite form
is a cluster of trees, willows perhaps,
or a field in fallow, going to grass.

It is this state of in between that counts.
So to claim that the Way is something more
than its parts is a full twist of the facts,

but to spend time on its strip, come about
each instant on its fine stretch – a good case
could be made for saying at least as much.

PETER ARMSTRONG

The Dean Surveys the Lingerie Dept.

Fifth column
   in a theocracy of woollens;
consider how the nave might entertain
   these metaphysical underwirings,
   the conceits of silk;
how the black spines of Prayer Books
   might nustle up this close against
an unreformed incense
   of satins and the skin.

(But these would be the master-craftsman's
   final and untouchable touches:
remember how we found her
   wrapped around the blind side of a screen
– his mistress' perfect likeness;
   that Godhead-blessing,
   unrepentant glimpse of thigh?)

O! Decorated of the flesh!
   Chartres of the curvatures!
Fan vault singing praises of the breast!
How many lenten disciplines
   might we come to love,
how many pure transcendent chills
if they teased us to epiphany?
– immanences, immanences;
   trappings of the rite.

SUJATA BHATT

One of Those Days

It was one of those days
when the silence made her
feel she could turn
into the marine algae
floating in her bath –

The sea salt and the tea-tree oil
soaked up by her skin
made her feel thirsty –

She could so easily turn
into the water itself, or
into the fragrant foam,
moving as if it belonged to an ocean.

And once down the drain
maybe she would find her way
to one of the true oceans:
the Pacific or the Indian –

Then the silence changed
and reminded her
of her other wish –
her desire to become a needle:
The sort chosen by a surgeon
at the very end, chosen to stitch up
the chest of an old man, for example,
after open-heart surgery.

It was one of those days
when the silence made it difficult
to know what to do

So she took the candle
from the table
and placed it on her head –
and she started to walk
around the kitchen.

The flame was a tongue of silk
licking the air to amber –
its blue root moving faster
        and faster –

As the hot wax dripped over
her hair, she closed her eyes
and imagined herself in the sauna:

Her spine almost singed against
the cedar – her face
close to the burning stones.

The candle was calm – she had
plenty of time – so she decided to go
upstairs to her room. Then, as she climbed
the steps, warmed by the swaying candle
                    on her head,
she thought of the snow outside,
                    the frozen rhododendron bushes –
and then she imagined herself as Surus.
Surus, Hannibal's last elephant –
his personal elephant, taken across
the Alps, over the snow –
Surus, the only elephant who lived
to carry Hannibal through the swamps –
But this time
she imagined Surus without Hannibal:

Surus being welcomed at the gates
and then managing
to explore Rome on his own –
The streets opening out new
possibilities at every corner –
Until, at last he would reach
          the market-place
where he would allow the children
to pet him and feed him grapes –

CHARLES BOYLE

Casual Work

When our children try to read between the lines
of our autograph books, we tell them about the year
the angels held their convention
at the Station Hotel.

Their debates on revisionist heresies
and minimum wingspans
passed over our heads, and we failed to seduce even one,
but we carried their Samsonite briefcases.

We fixed up the overhead projector.
We replenished their bottled water.
We recommended seafood restaurants.
We aired their rooms.

ALAN BROWNJOHN

Grain

Today sun, frost – and restlessness
      Room to room
I walked with my friend and our clinging shadows reached
Right out to the walls. But in the cellar's gloom
They couldn't find us, so we went untouched
Down the steps to look in a sheen of water,
Seeped in from the lake. At its edge – unsteady –
Shivering – I stopped. I sensed that ice might cover
Even these reflections soon, as the day turned cloudy,
And – *December*, I reflected, *month of my first*
Clear memory of winter . . .
      Back then, as well,
Shadows clung to us, boy and friend, dispersed
As we slipped them in the cellar. Skies were set to fall
Exactly as today. Now, too, I'll go
Back up alone to walk the road outside,
Take the touches of the dizzying dots of snow
On my held-out hand, think of loves and dreads and angers
As I did at seven.
      Frost and snow, unchanged, abide.
All that alters is the grain of my outstretched fingers
1999, 1939

JOHN BURNSIDE

Two Salisbury Sonnets

Unlookable for, by logic, by guess:
– W. H. Auden

Light

(after Constable)

In subtleties of colour: off-white, plum,
the almost-red of tiled rooves, or the wet
rainbow above the steeple; in the not
quite promised, or the covenant of some
unnamed degree of shade, we verge upon
the necessary presence. In the slant
of cloistered air, a wingspan, and the lit
magnetic pull of it: the shape that comes
and goes is nothing, absence, or the plain
fact of trees and horses, ley-lines that run
like murmurs through the soil, no more than rain
and fallen leaves. There's nothing to be seen
or only the shift from indigo to blue
we cannot grasp, approximate, and true.

Wood

And because this is also a forest:
acres of leaf and shadow and the calm
between each tide of birds; hectares of rain
and shelter; green men; wood-sprites we have lost
in practised or idle prayer; because some ghost
of mast and resin, risen from the grain
of oak or beech is written in the stone
for all to read, the old gods we have crossed
and still love, half-unwittingly, still dumb
with native wonder, come, from time to time,
to touch us in a doorway, breathe the dim
remembrance of themselves, on hair and skin
that passes from dust to dust, yet still belongs
to leaf and loam, essential and unknown.

CHARLES CAUSLEY

In Asciano

Detail, 'Adoration of the Shepherds'
– Pietro di Giovanni d'Ambrogio (1410–49)

Two Hodge-faced shepherds, having paid respects,
Appear uncertain as to what comes next.

An old man, white of hair, inclines his head
Uneasily, at something seen or said.

The way-worn girl beside him, winter-spare,
Draws close her cloak upon the candid air.

Back of a cattle-trough, doleful of eye
The statutory ox and ass stand by.

A small, bald baby, stiff and swaddled tight,
Absorbs the scene. His brow burns like a light.

Gawping, a dog appears from God-knows-where.
Halts in its path. Returns the infant stare.

What does it see? It drops a fearful jaw:
Raises, as though in self-defence, a claw.

The child rejoices at his risen day.
As for its ending, which of these shall say?

KATE CLANCHY

Feller, Son and Daughter

The child has never seen before
how big the farmyard creatures are:
he meets a pig's man-size,
appeasing stare, opens his mouth
to the unquacking duck, reaches out
a mittened paw to touch the gash
in the deer's dark fur. It's arched,
mid-leap, but with its head
and hooves cut off. He wants

to ask, but it's their turn, at last,
and Feller's man must check their chit,
and hook the Christmas turkey
down. He's bloodstained, expert,
kind. He tucks the bird
behind the pram, duveted in wax paper,
straps the wee boy snug in front,
grins, makes him a crown
of butcher's grass and holly.

The child shakes his fists and sings,
all the way home, *the five gold rings*,
chants to impervious feet
on shining streets, his list of lords,
French hens, and swans. It is
a litany of the near-extinct: beasts
known by name and husbanded,
birds falconed down, or shot and hung,
all butchered, paid, accounted for.

DAVID CONSTANTINE

School Parties in the Museum

Daily the boroughs, hopeful as a flood tide,
Release some children and Miss and Sir
And several guardian angels conduct them without loss
Through the underground in crocodiles to here,
The Room of the Kings, with questionnaires.

What the Jew Bloom said was no use – force,
Hatred, history, all that – here
There's enough of it to wipe out everything that lives,
Enough Fathers of the People, enough Peace Prize Winners
Among their deeds with a half-life of a million years.

Hurrying through from the Tea Room to the Reading Room
In drifts of children I could make no headway
But a space and a silence came into my mind
Among them crying like birds and flitting and settling
So that for once I saw a thing properly:

A thoughtful dot in socks and a white frock
Under the famous fist on its level length of arm,
Black granite fist, black as the people's blood is
When it has dried on the square in the usual sun,
Fist of some god or president, some wise

Dispenser of plagues of locusts and Agent Orange
And she was under it in pigtails with a clipboard
Pondering up at it in a space all on her own
As serious as the entire Reading Room
And black as a brand new question mark.

Daily for opening time and all day long
Till the last admission the ever hopeful boroughs send
Under the world's colours wave on wave
Of their bright fragments of the New Republic
Future present, with questions, against the Kings.

WENDY COPE

Fireworks Poem (One)

Faster and faster,
They vanish into darkness:
Our years together.

Fireworks Poem (Two)

Write it in fire across the night:
Some men are more or less all right.

ROBERT CRAWFORD

Mite

Let there be darkness, but not quite enough,
So it runs out before the job is done.

Praise be for shortfalls, loopholes and near-misses,
Leaps to the right conclusion, lives flung clear.

The saviour of the world was once as small
As $E=mc^2$ or a strawberry leaf.

Amen to the wee: loaves, fishes, needles' eyes.
Let the innocents be slaughtered. Except one.

DAVID DABYDEEN

Carnival Boy

not the still sad music of humanity
but a sound – rubber pun
steel, baton beating time to a lynched
nigger head – a sound that bangs out

child-glee

at what death is and what survives
now-now, never mind all that minstrelsy
and white abstraction:
intimations of immortality –
what survives is a sturdy unkillable boy
with a peasant's hard unblinking face
who grazes his sticks in meadows of steel

and plays the rhythms of what you have done
to others, what you will do to him
and he murmurs beforehand
but he knows too that when he shudders
the sticks will move his wrists
to eden fields, to his mother's hymns
which no man can stop when she is in full
brawling flow with Jesu each church
morning, – 'cause Jesu set we freeee
from sTavery
and we go sing clap hands and shake
we glad behinds, for no wand can con-
duct nor whip philosophize we

so he plays to his own blasted
rhythms, relishing his own survival:
the child is father of the pan.
fingers that barely scoop from bowl to mouth
will reach for the spiced sticks
to wrench the city's belly
so all along the tinsel tumble-
down streets of George Town or Spanish Town, hungry
people stepping out of line, hungry
people mashing and masking, hungry
people quilling their teeth.

AMANDA DALTON

Tuesdays

he'd catch the bus to visit her house,
stand opposite in the evening sun, or dark, or rain,
go home again on the number 22, or sometimes 23 or 17,
lay his tickets on the sideboard, dab a spot of glue
on the back and press them down in his book,
in tidy rows, like stamps or soldiers on parade.
Another month of this, he counted, he'd be on the final page.

PETER DIDSBURY

Not the Noise of the World

Not the noise of the world.
In the body of the whale
the system booms and roars
like pipework in
a broken-down hotel.

Not its spurious stillness.
In the limestone forest,
a soft declension
of calcined birds into ash.

No, not these,
but the complementaries,
brought and sought,
of sound and silence,
penitence and grace.

Birdsong occurring as gift in the vacuum
of the inter-canonical hours.

The silence made here,
conspired with here tonight,
as the silence of which
all liturgies are afraid.

MICHAEL DONAGHY

Tattoos

1

The serpent sheds her skin and yet
The pattern she'd as soon forgot
Recalls itself. By this I swear
I am the sentence that I bare.

2

Come years, poor thieves, and waste your time.
I never lock my door.
But in this sign, and by this rhyme,
I am your conqueror.

3

Copy this across your heart
And whisper what your eyes have heard
To summon me when we're apart
This spell made flesh, this flesh made word.

MAURA DOOLEY

Eclipse

There's something in my light: interference, distortion,
the razzle-dazzle of a foreign station,
stars in my eyes, dust, tears. Tune me in.
Make contact. The way his handkerchief
briefly, famously, once cleared her misty vision.

I try to read but – kaleidoscope, stroboscope,
magic lantern – before my very eyes the world
breaks up. Words lose their pattern of
country, continent, ocean and scatter
alphabets, archipelagoes of loose language.

I'm not Saint Lucy, who tore out her eyes
the better to see. I will not be blinded by love,
the delusions of my age. Lend me your glasses.
Pass the telescope. I'll stuff these lenses in
so as not to miss the passing of this heavenly body.

CAROL ANN DUFFY

–/–/99

Postman, postman, be as slow as you like
delivering this, your wobbling bike
barked down city streets, round country bends,
on your back a sack, bulging
with all our whispering, singing, yelling words
as the twentieth century ends.

IAN DUHIG

American Graffiti

I. Women's Room

I open for you my mouth. I open for you
My two eyes, the white chambers of my skull;
From my old tongue, your sentences will rise
For I am Goddess Tlaelquani, Eater of Excrement,
Sister of Tlazolteotl. Problems with your partner?
I cut off his eggs with my obsidian glass knife.
Perhaps your employer is harrassing you?
I gut him and stuff the corpse with chocolate.
Maybe a cab-driver has overcharged you?
I sacrifice his first-born to the Plumed Serpent.
See? I've a knack for this sort of thing
And you worship me just by sitting here,
A grudge at your breast, adjusting the mask.
My mouth is closed. Open your mouth. Ask.

II. Men's Room

Your look flickers across disinfected surfaces,
Starting from all eye-contact as if it burned
For this is the time and temple of reflection,
Of Tlaelquani's sister, I, great Tlazolteotl,
Goddess of scum and the skeletons in their closets.
Should I lick the half-moon on my thumbnail,
Your manhood's index weeps itself to death
Like a candle running down a feast day skull.
This image degrades men, it's true, but I light
Everything they think they've got away with,
The footprints of liars where they first fell:
Hell creeps back up them to you like a slow fuse
And it won't be enough to piss on your shoes.

HELEN DUNMORE

Ice Coming

(after Doris Lessing)

First, the retreat of bees
lifting, heavy with the final
pollen of gorse and garden,
lugging the weight of it, like coal sacks
heaped on lorry-backs
in the ice-cream clamour of August.

The retreat of bees, lifting
all at once from city gardens –
suddenly the roses are scentless
as cold probes like a tongue,
crawling through the warm crevices
of Kew and Stepney. The ice comes
slowly, slowly, not to frighten anyone.

Not to frighten anyone. But the Snowdon
valleys are muffled with avalanche,
the Thames freezes, the Promenades des Anglais
clinks with a thousand icicles, where palms
died in a night, and the sea
of Greece stares back like stone
at the ice-Gorgon, white as a sheet.

Ice squeaks and whines. Snow slams
like a door miles off, exploding a forest
to shards and matchsticks. The glacier
is strangest, grey as an elephant,
too big to be heard. Big-foot, Gorgon –
a little mythology
rustles before it is stilled.

So it goes. Ivy, mahonia, viburnum
lift their fossilised flowers
under six feet of ice, for the bees
that are gone. As for being human
it worked once, but for now
and the foreseeable future
the conditions are wrong.

DOUGLAS DUNN

Dinner

Hungry for too long, the first hot spoonful
Juddered me with its sudden soothe and taste.
I huddled over the aroma of minestrone
As if in a soup kitchen in a charity coat,
Thankful and blessed by circumstance while also
Alert to my companion's dainty attack,
He being well fed, quicker, his expectations
Satisfied to the minute in his happier routines.
Slowly, with gratitude, I emptied the plate,
Wiped it with bread, drank down my wine and water.
I could eat no more, nor ordered it.
My companion did, he with the appetite,
Security and confident conversation.
He was too hungry, or not hungry enough,
Ignorant of the gluttonies of aloneness
Which are frugal fare, the small meal prepared,
Half eaten, cleaned away, the empty table,
Four hopeful chairs, and life without kiss.

U. A. FANTHORPE

Words for Months

Their names in this country
Wore out, though the weather
Is still what they charted:

After-Yule; Mud-month; Mad
(The one that wants to knock
You down and plant a tree

On top of you); Easter
(Her month, the spring lady);
Three-milkings-a-day month

(Everyone smelling of
Cow); First-nice-month; Second-
Nice (our fathers had no

Word for spade but spade); Weed;
Holy; Leaf-fall; Shambles
(Cattle-culling month); and

Here-we-are-again Yule.

Someone has overlaid
This tired chronicle
Of endless days, thin lives

With shoddy Roman goods –
War, doorways, emperors,
Even the numbers wrong.

They fit better, the dull
Words for difficult things:
Mud. Milk. Weeds. Leaf-fall. Cull.

Se aeftera Geola; Sol-monath; Hreth-monath; Easter-monath;
Thrimylce; Se aerra Litha; Se aeftera Litha; Weod-monath;
Halig-monath; Winter-fylleth; Blot-monath; Se aerra Geola.

(from W. W. Skeat, *A Student's Pastime*, 1896)

PAUL FARLEY

Fly

Hardly anything, a fine-winged fly on the window pane,
one of the day's ten-thousand seconds captured,
made visible. Inconsequential, its moments in the world
squandered on this wall of light it can't surmount,

far from water. It must have got in overnight
through one of those chinks we don't like to admit
to owning – with our campaigns of strip-blinds,
                                        insect-o-cutors
and arsenic paper, you could say we haven't got on,

that you remind us of something we'd rather forget;
some thread of trial and error, intricate
and long since perfected, fully working before we arrived
on the scene at one minute to midnight; that you knew

summers of the smaller hours, Venusian seasons
and still go through the whole thing on bus shelter roofs,
canals, anywhere warm and wet enough. Can you see me
fly; a castellated, bloodshot eye, day's growth

and did you see me enter, or feel the slammed air
then a settling through the house, silence again
and onwards in your slow ascent from the sill
against the dawn's skin, gorged a red that you see in waves.

Up close, you've spat on your hands, that same solving rub
when faced with sashes, great bays, or top decks of buses
the world over, baffled in our era of glass
that you slip against time and again, en route for an edge

though it's strange the way you'll so readily accept a frame,
tracing an algebra of infinite confinement,
a treatise on the lack of straight lines in nature,
that hard-bitten philosophy found in cage birds

and aquaria; a pattern I've seen displayed
on skylights, shithouse walls, the pelts of dead dogs;
or trapped in famine footage, a matte blip
that kept Lindbergh awake as he crossed the Atlantic

again and again in a film. The east has grown bright.
In your register of time I have held my pen
steadily for hours. In mine, all I have to say
is brushed to one side as I give up writing this,

take a fly-age to cross the room, draw back the lace;
to lift up the latch, encourage you with one sharp breath,
the air catching your wings, letting noun become verb,
and you join the world of things, of everything being the case.

VICKI FEAVER

Speech

Like snow – melting
as it reaches the streets –

leaving less mark
than the viscous

path of a snail;
or surviving

as a ribbon
of raised dots

passing through
the fingers

of blind angels,
feeling their way

from baby talk
to dying croak,

laughing
and weeping.

ROY FISHER

And On That Note:

Jazz Elegies

Wellstood, for forty-odd years,
guessed what there was to do next
and did it. Tipped
the history of the art half over
and went in where it suited;
and understanding that music's
more about movement than structure
proceeded to lurch, stamp,
splash, caper, grumble, sprint,
bump and trudge – mostly
on the piano – then sat down
in his hotel room before dinner
and, too soon, stopped.

Strange channels for new noises. That steely-eyed
old man, dapper,
sugar-coated in famous vanity
and endless glad-handing,
carried always somewhere about him
what he'd come upon early, a monstrous,
husky, thoroughly dangerous saxophone sound
never before heard on earth;
and on a bandstand if you put your foot
behind him hard enough,
out it would still come honking
with no manners at all.

Three piano-players
taking turns on the portable
stool. The first
tucks it close in
and perches like a hamster, as he must.
Second, I slide it back
to make good room to slouch
as I permit myself. Finally,
gaunt and purposeful, he drags it
to the extreme: Glenn Gould
plays Crazy Horse in crimson suede
pointed boots; extensible arms
reaching for distant keys, spine curved,
navel in phobic flight from the piano. The music,
after a moment's meditation, comes streaking out
in elasticated pulses: wild, dramatic,
timeless East European Stride

Taking care never to learn
the ways of the world till the moment
the alto would assume its insinuating angle and get
blown straight into life. Seeing a waiting audience, then
blinking awake mildly, leaning down to whisper
surprise news to the pianist: 'Trouble is,
I just can't seem to remember the names of
any tunes at all. Serious problem there.' Prolonged
pause, prolonged. Again, after some painful night:
'How can those people go on playing
for twenty or thirty years and never even
start to want to learn their instruments?'
Serious question there.

Ears up, neck solid,
punching pretty tunes off centre
through a stubby *cornett*: 'The way I figure it,
the sound comes out
that much closer to my face, and
that's where I want it.' Lovely old
American tunes, and talking: 'I guess you people
must all be thinking I'm just another American
loudmouth!' Talking: 'What key?
THIS key!' 'What tempo?
It's a BALLAD, for Christ's sake!' On a sofa
at a party in his honour, persuaded
to toot gently and graciously for his supper,
looses off at full volume and quells
New York Town Hall, with nothing
in pursuit but my quite small piano.

Whistling in the dark
wobbling a pallid flame down
to the bottom of the bottle:
owl-sounds, muffled
squawks. Nothing
better to do but whistle
when there's so much dark.

This poem commemorates some musicians, now dead, I used to
play with, or alongside: Bud Freeman, Archie Semple, Duncan Swift,
Dick Wellstood, Bruce Turner, Wild Bill Davison.

JOHN GLENDAY

Genesis

The United Materialist Church believes
that at any given moment God demolishes the world,
only to rebuild it instantly, altered and oblivious.

Everything from our first formlessness
to the final blare of light stands witness
to this infinite substantiation of His love.

Their bible consists of just the one book,
predictably named Genesis.
Here we may read of that strange bush consumed

in a terrible caul of silence; and the lost garden,
without fruit and without serpent,
where the hopeful naked wait with the hopeful innocent.

LAVINIA GREENLAW

The Spirit of the Staircase

In our game of flight, half-way down
was as near mid-air as it got: a point
of no return we'd fling ourselves at
over and over, riding pillows or trays.
We were quick to smooth the edge
of each step, grinding the carpet
to glass on which we'd lose our grip.
The new stairs were our new toy,
the descent to an odd extension,
our four new rooms at flood level
in the sunken garden – a wing
dislocated from a hive. Young bees
with soft stripes and borderless nights,
we'd so far been squared away
in a twin-set of bunkbeds, so tight-knit,
my brother and I once woke up finishing
a conversation begun in a dream.
It had been the simplest exchange,
and one I'd give much to return to:
the greetings of shadows, unsurprised
at having met beneath the trees
and happy to set off again, alone,
back into the dark.

ANDREW GREIG

A Night Rose

There is a balance in the conservatory of the soul . . .
– Erzebet Szanto

When her moment came
in the deep of night,
she reached out and handed it to me:

a Night Rose.
Black and radiant as the centre of an eye,
you've no idea how rare.

It rests now on
an unreachable shelf.
I think we put it there.

From time to time she writes
she's felt another petal fall.
She would not have me say where.

Petal for petal, magic and loss:
let them for once
weigh exactly the same with us.

SOPHIE HANNAH

Long For This World

I settle for less than snow,
try to go gracefully like seasons go

which will regain their ground –
ditch, hill and field – when a new year comes round.

Now I know everything:
how winter leaves without resenting spring,

lives in a safe time frame,
gives up so much but knows he can reclaim

all titles that are his,
fall out for months and still be what he is.

I settle for less than snow:
high only once, then no way up from low,

then to be swept from drives.
Ten words I throw into your changing lives

fly like ten snowballs hurled:
I hope to be, and will, long for this world.

DAVID HARSENT

from *Marriage*

I perch on a 'Bauhaus-style' chrome and raffia
stool as you drop your knife and pause to consider
this fish and its fistula,

this fish with its deep deformity, its head like a cosh,
its raw flank and blood-brown eyes,
its lips of lopsided blubber,

this fish we are having for supper.
You laid out cold cash
to have them deliver this fish, close-packed in ice,

a glacier coelacanth preserved against all the odds,
as if some throw of the dice, some coin
turning a thousand years to come down heads,

had brought to the marble slab in our kitchen
of all kitchens this fish, sporting
its jowly truncheon-lump of sorbo rubber

and the great wet ulcer opening beneath its backbone.
As you start again, flensing good from bad, you let spill
a viscous flub of gut that slips

from your wrist to the marble, where it spells
out the hierogram most often linked
with the once in a lifetime, miraculous

descent of the goddess, her gills
crisp enough to cut as you trade kiss for kiss.
Flesh of her flesh. I'll eat it if you will.

W. N. HERBERT

Lines on the West Face of Salisbury Cathedral

(whilst concealed for restoration)

1

Who are your saints?
Who would you set
in the unoccupied niche
after niche that lifts
into a losing heart?

Where did our souls get to,
those urgent notions, freed
from oaks, glimpsed like owls,
those stand-ins for the pose
that holds forever?

How did we come to care
so much for the blankness
that succeeds us to
seek out, beg and win
this space that's listening?

2

Here are my latest martyrs:
Saint David Ginola,
Saint Billie Mackenzie,
Saint Julie Burchill,
Saint Bjork, Saint Buster.

None did the usual miracles
but all, for years or hours
or instants, acted with
that huge and comic grace
that seems to hold us here.

Who are your saints?
Who would you set
in the unoccupied niche
after niche that lifts
into a changing heart?

3

Arriving in rain or to
a totality of air
stare at this cancelled space
where saints should rank
like pines upon a hillside
and ask its shroud for insight.

What is the point of massing
love, like minutes into years,
as though this was a forest
you climbed like a child,
as though you suckled from
the many-breasted stone?

I think we must have come here
because the past adores us.

TRACEY HERD

Black Swan

An English garden, its lakes and lawns,
a *corps de ballet* of pale roses,
the drifting mid-winter of swans.

She is lost in her shifting reflection.
The miniature bridge is stiffly arched
in its heavy slipper of stone.

Gone is the dark-haired, dark-eyed Russian
girl, bare-faced, black hair scraped back
from her aristocratic bones

who would sit mutely with her swans.
Her breath tears at her throat
in a feverish spray of thorns.

In an empty theatre, the bouquets are strewn,
the elaborate costumes carefully hung
backstage in the many-mirrored room.

The sky darkens behind its stars.
A frozen moon defines
the black swan rising from the lake.

SELIMA HILL

Arkansasoline

Everywhere I go I collect them.
I've done it all my life. I can't resist.
I take them home like eggs and inspect them
and lay them out like this. If this were thist.
On the bus I meet a cross *standee*.
And in the nursing-home a *brigadoon*.
The council-chambers boast a fine *grandee*
Red is *cochineal*, blue *lagoon*.
The great James Joyce maintains the most 'euphonious'
is *cellar-door*. The one *I* like is *coolly*.
Or is the hypen – hyphen-'door' – erroneous?
Should coolly have a hyphen? (Unlike wool-ly.)
Is gas pronounced like gore when it's not gasoline?
Is Arkansas the short for Arkansasoline?

TOBIAS HILL

Later

All night she keeps the car radio on,
driving from station to station. Bhangra,
long waves, small voices, *Walking on the Moon*.
In the morning it is all behind her

and light comes shearing through the southern rain.
She stops to take pictures of a rainbow,
the span of it above the contraflow
quite still, as if nothing has yet fallen,

not her out of her life nor this downpour
through all the colours of the sky. Layby
daffodils wave their hollow heads at her,
bent back. Lifting. She thinks of poetry.

Beautiful things. The perfect words you say
only later, too late, driving away.

MICHAEL HOFMANN

The Doppler Effect

Three days since my last big girl's overdose.
'Coffee?' 'Er, no thank you.' A couple of Germans
are chatting up a couple of escort agency escorts.
Pikant. My wedding ring has gone awol.
My wife has gone awol, and sits opposite,
making heavy weather of her pudding. I break off
a piece of panforte. When I could be playing
paper scissors stone with my little boy.

MICK IMLAH

1860

By the shore of Lake Constance I sat down and prayed
That your health should not collapse in an African swamp.
I found the name you carved before I was born
On the Tower of Pisa, and chiselled mine beneath it.
When our hotel in Brussels burned to the ground,
I fled with nothing but my bullfinch and your portrait, dear.

Two dreams: that you have come home at last
With your throat slit, and walk by me without speaking;
Or, as I roam the poor quarters of Mecca or Medina
In my loose nightgown, exhausted with yearning,
I cry aloud, 'Does he care for me?' –
And think I hear an angel whisper, 'Yes'.

KATHLEEN JAMIE

Hoard

What kind of figure did he cut
out there in the dusk, gut-wound
packed with sphagnum,
as he sank into the bog
his offering of weaponry,
blades courteously broken,
his killed cherished swords?

ALAN JENKINS

Her Last Nightdress

A cotton one with a few flowers and a bit of lace
at the neck, her name stitched inside, it falls
from my bag of socks and shirts and smalls
and looks so innocent, so out of place
I see her again, hot and flustered in the ward

we took her to, and helpless, late at night
when even she admitted 'something wasn't right'
and I left her waving, and she sort of smiled
to say I mustn't worry, must get on,
get back, to sleep, to work, to my important life.

Next day, I went to M&S, I bought
the nightdress she had asked for as an afterthought
and took it to her, and she put it on
and loved it – no more the sad, unreconciled,
bewildered woman I had fought, no more

my father's tetchy, disappointed wife;
girlish, almost. She wore it for a while
until one day I walked in and she was lying there
in a hospital gown, so starched and plain
and this pretty one had gone into her drawer –

the something that was wrong had made a stain,
a stench I took away with me somehow
to wash, and forgot all about till now
I stand here in the warm soap-smelling air
but can't think why, and sob, and people stare.

JACKIE KAY

Smoking Under Stars

At night, when the moon waits right
at my back door, where I stand
smoking under healthy stars,
every dead person has the same dead face.
The moon's big mug has watched them all.
Not missed a trick, not a single death.
Not the dead woman in the pine box
in the tall pine lands of Scotland,
or the dead man lying on the wooden table
in the small orange village in Nigeria.
She died, Margaret Baxter, wondering
if things were just the same or changed.
The way she peeled a potato hadn't changed at all.
But the potatoes had. Jesus, more names
for potatoes than the names of her sisters.
Irene, Annie, Agnes – three.
When she died, she watched her whole past
float before her –
scrubbed and white and yellow, knuckled,
in a basin with cold water and potato peelings.
And she tried to remember her own name.
And the name of the black man with the dancing eyes who
went away who went away who went away.
I am just waiting. I have their deaths inside me.
The moon knows all about it.

MIMI KHALVATI

The Fabergé Egg

It is born as a shape, the shape of birth.
  Always the same shape but no sooner born
Than form, the buried form spring must unearth,
  Must make new, however timeless or timeworn,
Calls to its maker: 'What am I, what am I
  Beyond my shell? Am I fish or fowl, flower
    Or fruit, whose roots are these, whose clay? What lies
          In my white mortuary,
  Rocking, crowning through slippages that shower
    Stones on my head?' And its maker replies:

'These are the hands I have trained for you, these
  Their veins. Running across the grain, so thin
Not one runs straight. Let them run with the ease
  Of grasses, tendrils, stems, over the skin
I stretch for you, look, against the light, fine
  As pink enamel, how the sun's glow steals
    Through each soft web, soft as a fontanelle.
          See how its candles shine?'
  Form nods its head. And each nod breaks, peals
    Into a lily of the valley bell.

Bells so true to life, life's put in the shade.
　　'In these fonts I'll christen you in ablutions
Of gold rivers, turn you through ruby, jade,
　　Diamond, pearl, rockcrystal revolutions.
And under the crown that will spread your fame
　　With three Easter kisses, a "Christ is risen",
　　　"Yes Christ is truly risen", I'll install
　　　　　　Heads in a threefold frame.
　　Who but a goldsmith would think to imprison
　　　Their likenesses in such a small cathedral!

The Czarina, she'll thank me for it. Olga,
　　Tatiana, their father Nicholas . . .
As for these hands that work as well in vulgar
　　Gunmetal, on copper pots, nickel, brass
Shell casings and grenades – it's not your hoard
　　Or your precious stones a new world will praise
　　　When a mother's love has bitten the dust
　　　　　　And you're banished abroad
　　But these, their skill.' There's no response. Buds raise
　　　Their heads and hang them. Droop as lilies must.

TOM LEONARD

Fireworks Poems

I. Socialist Utopian Fireworks Poem

over the moon

a level playing field

at the end of the day

I would like this to catch the child's picture-book lettering, quite simply and clearly. Each line should appear in sequence, preferably to leave all three in the sky.

II. Autumn Sky Fireworks Poem

coruscating capella

*

steady-eyed venus

o

By the end of August, Capella is low in the horizon as a brilliantly coruscating star going through the prismatic colours. (By January it is high in the sky as a steady bright light.) In this autumn it is in coruscating mode, with Venus, the brightest planet, also visible.

III. Food for Thought

a mush

room

c
l
o
u
d

MICHAEL LONGLEY

The Beech Tree

Leaning back like a lover against this beech tree's
Two-hundred-year-old pewter trunk, I look up
Through skylights into the leafy cumulus, and join
Everybody who has teetered where these huge roots
Spread far and wide our motionless mossy dance,
As though I'd begun my eclogues with a beech
As Virgil does, the brown envelopes unfolding
Like fans their transparent downy leaves, tassels
And prickly cups, mast, a fall of vermilion
And copper and gold, then room in the branches
For the full moon and her dusty lakes, winter
And the poet who recollects his younger self
And improvises a last line for the georgics
About snoozing under this beech tree's canopy.

RODDY LUMSDEN

Makeover

The way my hand might fail to draw your head
starting with an oval, sketching in
two godforsaken eyeholes halfway down,
then nose and lips, a wonky chin
but still might add a perfect, painted crown
of hair, each hair, in Titian red;

is that the way the Scouse hairdresser
presided over you that day the BBC
brought you to the Kensington Hotel
to make you over,
much like a preacher scrubbing up to oversee
some Catholic or gnostic ritual?

I can imagine, by his side, at prayer,
St Cosmas and St Damian, twin brothers
and patron saints of hairdressers and barbers,
who had their heads lopped off, but felt no pain.
And representing bigger hair,
the patron saint of stylists, Mary Magdalene.

And so the cutter took his Joewell scissors
to your split ends (a pair is worth
a whole month's wages to a salon junior
with scabbed and scaly hands from endless washing).
He pegged your fringe back to the season's length,
and gave his blessing

then sat you in the climazone
and finished off the style beneath the rollerball.
The taxi man they organised to drive you home
misheard and thought you were Sinéad O'Connor.
I was in the kitchen with your dinner
and let you know you hadn't changed at all.

SARAH MAGUIRE

The Florist's at Midnight

Stems bleed into water
  loosening their sugars
    into the dark,

clouding dank water
  stood in zinc buckets
    at the back of the shop.

All night the chill air
  is humid with breath.
    Pools of it mist

from the dark mouths
  of blooms,
    from the agape

of the last arum lily –
  as a snow-white wax shawl
    curls round its throat

cloaking the slim yellow tongue,
  with its promise of pollen,
    solitary, alert.

Packed buckets
  of tulips, of lilies, of dahlias
    spill down from tiered shelving

nailed to the wall.
  Lifted at dawn,
    torn up from their roots

then cloistered in cellophane,
   they are cargoed across continents
      to fade far from home.

How still they are
   now everyone has gone,
      rain printing the tarmac

the streetlights
   in pieces
      on the floor.

GLYN MAXWELL

The Paving Stones

Between a spring and the river with a name
there'll be a place it turns or the water flinches,
    is barely ruffled, wouldn't dream
of whitening, has run on, smoothed its silk out
but has been clipped, and you in a 'sixties style

stroller let your head bow down, your chin
lodge on the rail your mittens hold and your eyes
    watch the parading space and line
and space and line recur in the paving stones
this close below. It mills and mesmerises,

and you still have it, earlier than a sound,
sweet as either hand: through the long days
    it scurries under, still a ground
passing. If you stain it for a moment,
it means to say, a line is what arises.

ROGER McGOUGH

The Wrong Beds

(after Baudelaire)

Life is a hospital ward, and the beds we are put in
are the ones we don't want to be in.
We'd get better sooner if put over by the window.
Or by the radiator, one could suffer easier there.

At night, the impatient soul dreams of faraway places.
The Aegean: all marble and light. Where, upon a beach
as flat as a map, you could bask in the sun like a lizard.

The Pole: where, bathing in darkness, you could watch
the sparks from Hell reflected in a sky of ice.
The soul could be happier anywhere than where it happens
to be.

Anywhere but here. We take our medicine daily,
nod politely, and grumble occasionally.
But it is out of our hands. Always the wrong place.
We didn't make our beds, but we lie in them.

MEDBH McGUCKIAN

Our Lady's Bedstraw

Mary sweetens it out, it blows
into an Irish half-moon. Like a cross
maltreated on a hill it gives him shelter.

It is the pairing bed of heaven to his soul,
an eye-well which dyes his limbs black,
and holds him honoured in its songless web.

In the border-hours his one-voiced cry
through the hearting rock of the wall
lights a third window trees ache towards.

JAMIE McKENDRICK

Good Hedges

He wants the holly tree cut down to size,
the holly tree where the birds are sound, and safe
from his cat whose snickering impersonation
of birdsong – more like the din a mincer makes –
fools no-one, and charms nothing out of the trees.

He wants us to tidy up the pyracantha sprouting
its fire-thorns and berry-laden fractals, and clip
the brambles, the lilacs, everything wild.
Next he'll want the hedgehog's spikes filed down,
the mole's claws bound up with green twine

– already he's replaced his own hair with ginger nylon.
His light he says is being blocked. It's dark
where he is. He has a point – so many deaths
in these few houses, it's like something
loosëd from the bible. One lucky escape, though:

the bearded roofer, one along, who lost
his footing, high on the scaffolding, and fell,
with his deck of tiles, on his shoulder and skull.
Sometimes tears come to his eyes for no reason
he can think of, but now the sun's out he sits again

on the patio, plucking from his banjo
some Appalachian strand of evergreen bluegrass
then an Irish reel where his fingers scale
a glittering ladder like a waterfall
so even the songbirds hush in the holly tree.

PAULA MEEHAN

Ectopic

The four full moons of the yellow sky
pulsate. Four full moons and I need
morphine. I need more morphine to stop the hurting.

I would gut my granny for another hit.
Someone's sewn me up and left the kitchen tap,
the apple Mac, a rabid bat, a handy anvil

inside me. The stitches there above the mons
(*Won't interfere with the bikini line . . .*) neat
as my own white teeth clenched and grinding in pain,

that grin up, second mouth!, at the ceiling lights, the
                                                    moons! and
I will work out their complicated orbits
relative to the sun and why the stars have

all deserted me. I want to know the weight

of my little creature's soul and why its fate

has been to leave before I had a chance to save
her. Or him. It? They keep calling it *it*.
I am a woman with a sieve carrying sand

from the beach. And all this time the rain
is hammering the window pane. I count perfect feet.
Your ten perfect toes. Your perfect fingers ten. Your blue
                                                    eyes, since,

perfect foetus, I must summon up the will to kill
you soon before you get too strong a grip
on the black hole that occupies the void that was my heart.

O somewhere there is a beautiful myth of sorting,
of sifting through a mountain of dross to find the one seed
whose eventual blossom is such would make a god cry.

ADRIAN MITCHELL

Orpheus with the Beasts and Birds

(based on a painting by Roelandt Savery
in the Fitzwilliam Museum, Cambridge)

Guitar in his hands
Leaning on an Elephant
Orpheus sings

A Wolfhound and St Bernard
At his knees

A grey Ox
Cocks his ear

Two Swans
Lift their snaking heads
Towards the music

The Geese are paddling in the shallows
Gathering peppery green weeds

A flowering Ostrich on a rock
Throws back her wings
In ecstasy

The Waterfall bounces
Silver notes

A Leopard reclining
Like a streamlined blonde

A Lion and Lioness
Roll their golden eyes

A Heron taking off
On a journey to the hidden stars

The Peacock flaunts
His starry blue
Waterfall of a tail

A million Birds
In proud mid-flight
Scattering their colours
All over the sky

A lurking Buffalo
With guilty eyes

A family of Deer
Guarding each other with their branches

Birds and Animals
Feeding   Drinking
Singing   Resting

The Trees are dancing
Stretching and swirling
And the Sky is a dance
Of speeding blue and white

It is all a dance
And at its centre
The wedding of two Horses
They have a special temple
Of grass and flowers
Among the shining rocks

The Grey Horse looks at me
The Chestnut turns away
Their flanks are touching
Silver flank against
Chestnut flank
Two Horses
So glad and close together
It can only be love

Never lose it

Guitar in his hands
Leaning on an Elephant
Orpheus sings

I lost her once
I lost her twice
I lost her once
In Paradise

Eurydice
Eurydice

I lost her once
I lost her twice
In a dark tunnel
Made of ice

Eurydice
Eurydice

I looked back
And for the second time she died
Oh grief comes in and out like the tide

Eurydice
Eurydice

Guitar in his hands
Leaning on an Elephant
Orpheus sings

EDWIN MORGAN

The Demon Judges a Father

Antony, Antony! Antony of the desert!
There are caves everywhere, caves for beasts.
There are white ruins half buried in the sand,
Bleached dead but for flies, a bat or two,
Scuttle of a scorpion in the shimmer.
There is dung. Someone lives here. Yes!
It is only a huddle of black, with a hood,
Eyes like gimlets, crouched in a doorway,
Streaked with dust, missing nothing,
Desert father, father of nothing,
Antony! He stirs and shifts and spits,
Withdraws a swarthy ancient finger
From somewhere in his robe, points at me
With an undisguised menace as if battalions
Of invisibles were itching at his command
To cut me down. Not a chance! The flies
He irritably shakes from sipping his brow
Are back at once. He is himself besieged
By an army of sorts, prowling, preening, prancing
Among the chicken-bones and balls of shit:
Trunkless men and fish-tailed women,
Arses on wheels, arses with flutes in them,
Eggs on legs, pigs with wigs, sheela-na-gigs,
Giant red-mantled rats, dwarfs with zimmers –
What a trauchle of temptations and torments!
The monstrous dance of forms is all his,
It has not come from outer space, it is

The cess and soss and process of his selfhood.
Ah you saint you, you solitary non-server
Of the people, your persecutors are shadows
Because you persecute yourself. Shadow
Of a man, you have lost the coat of many colours.
Oh how you hate the brightnesses of the world!
Dig your heels in the sand and scowl. I know
You won't speak to me: you think I am virtual.
But I'm not one of your monsters, I am real.
I can stare you out. I do stare you out.
You are yourself a desert, and I've done with you.

BLAKE MORRISON

Against Dieting

Please, darling, no more diets.
I've heard the talk on why it's
good for one's esteem. I've watched you
jogging lanes and pounding treadmills.
I've even shed two kilos of my own.
But enough. What are love-handles
between friends? For half a stone
it isn't worth the sweat.
I've had it up to here with crispbread.
I doubt the premise too.
Try to see it from my point of view.
I want not less but more of you.

ANDREW MOTION

Flint

I ask you: how can you maintain
there is no life or feeling in a stone?

I have this flint in my hand: look.
In two bits it might be a heart that broke.

PAUL MULDOON

The Breather

Think of this gravestone
as a long, low chair
strategically placed
at a turn in the stair.

EILÉAN NÍ CHUILLEANÁIN

To the Angel in the Stone

Trampled in the causeway, the stone the builders passed over
Cries out: 'Bone of the ranked heights', from darkness
Where moss and spiders never venture,
'You know what ways I plumbed, past what hard threshold,

'You see our affliction, you know
How we were made, how we decay. At hand
When the backbone crashed in the sea tide, you have heard
How the waves are breaking our bones.

'You look down where the high peaks are ranging,
You see them flickering like flames –
They are like a midge dancing at evening.

'Give me rest for a day, let me mourn,
Let me lie on the stone bench above the tree-tine
And drink water for one whole day.'

GRACE NICHOLS

Cosmic Disco

While stars explode
   on the dancefloor of infinity,
      spinning out of the milky way
            into new galaxies

For the Sun, in flamingo dress,
it's a case of burn Baby burn
and every planet worth its salt,
even the rings of Saturn,
all swirl and swirl.

Meanwhile, back on chart-topping earth,
     everything too, in purposeful motion,
         the rocking-with-the-wind trees,
           the moon-dancing ocean.

And out on the disco floor,
under the shifting fortunes
of the disco lights,

Stars are exploding again,
    grouping and regrouping
         into new constellations,

This time, it's the phosphorus-girls
doing the orbiting,
the funky cygnus-looping,

One eye on the gravitational-boys,
one eye on the indispensable
satellites of their handbags.

SEAN O'BRIEN

Law

I was proceeding in an easterly direction
When the vehicle stopped beside me and I saw
The driver brandishing a kitchen knife.
The passenger was struggling with the door.
So naturally I sought to intervene then
By asking what the silverware was for,
But through the glass the driver would not listen.
The passenger, meanwhile, was on the floor
And gouts of blood were jumping at the windscreen.
Though disinclined to witness any more,
I tried – because I hope I know my duty –
To understand this work of tooth and claw,
And having watched, I'm driven to conclude
That murder is the engine of the law.

BERNARD O'DONOGHUE

Philomela

If things got any worse, she'd take up knitting
And sit across the hearth from his thin-lipped silence,
Murmuring a new language and logic:
*Cast on purlwise. Knit one stitch through back
Of loop. Yarn round needle. C6B, P6, K2.*
And it would all mean nothing to him,
Such woman's writing. No more than love had.

So what should the picture on her peplum be?
On the whole, a sorry scene: not exactly
A tongue cut out, but the steady rooting up
Of a grove of voices, one after the other.
And as her fingers filled the details in,
His hawkish eyes will fill with tears, hearing
Her absent humming from across the fire.

RUTH PADEL

Hey Sugar, Take a Walk on the Wild Side

Imagine we're two bottles of Strozzapieto
Di Padrone Olive Oil, the pond-green
      sluggish stuff, WD40 with pips
that slipped their way down in the soil
of the Bay of Naples fifty years ago

and witched themselves into that silvery
upward pour of antique, bullet-proof, really
      goodlooking bark. He didn't know he had them,
the guy in the deli. They got pushed together
by an unknown hand in his basement store –

twin litres of Biba nail-varnish, untouchably
black-green. He sets them side by side
      on the highest shelf as Ivy Street lights go on
to preside over tins of Shark Fin Soup, Almond
Parfait Supreme, his Lavender Liquorice Rods.

Here we are, look, alone, a jewelly secret,
Hansel and Gretel in Aladdin's cave
      of Cupressa *Dolmades*, looking down from the gods
on Banana Conserve and Vintage Marmalade
plus a Rumpelstiltskin heap of Farmhouse Gold.

Never mind tomorrow's big opening, blinds
flying up on us. Whatever the future holds,
      we've got these pistachio truffles and ruffles,
these rowdy ripples of cranberry vinegar
all to ourselves. Sssh, darling, our night has come.

TOM PAULIN

Sarum's Prize

'Its spire a poplar or an aspen leaning against the wind,
yet firm as a rock.'

Because the style called Romanes-
que buckles under pressure
– those dull round arches
are dense
like nougatine or fudge
– they never tense
because that style won't budge
English Gothic took the stress
– it simply had to
freeborn noble quirky
its impassioned gestures
burst like water from the water meadows
into something graceful and jerky

spring sprang or sprung rhythm
an entirely new measure
leapt out of that dark backward abysm
– yes the past is always murky
and in its fountainy *virtù*
that new rhythm
– rhythm and jaggy mass
made a permanent surprise
that Master Elias
his builders and his masons chose
as Sarum's prize

but as rough canvas has the right tooth for some
driven desperate painters
or yacking consonants clipe the ears
of riven poets
– clipe or clasp like jism
kicking for the ovum
so Gothic's a style like frett-
y chervil – that is organic
like a salad
even though its mystery and dread
echo that mix of *no* and *yes*
that is the light
– the freakish splintery bursting risky light
rising out of chaos darkness
and old – that is too ancient – night

KATHERINE PIERPOINT

It Went By Very Fast

'I saw the moon, but it went by very fast
when I was in a rocket,'
says the child.

He's ringed by play's rubble;
crayons, stickers, pebbles, sweets,
discarded experiments fall
round the foot of his chair
like lopped hair at the barber's.

His hands are always moving, as eyes do;
fingers working, feeling,
they feed the mind.

'A rocket flies so fast
all the people in it go backwards.'

He's at home with truth,
it rides him lightly, worldmaking.

Something went by me once,
I thought – *it went by very fast* –
diamond drillpoint
of one streamer through the head,
that truth; it flew so fast, it sparked
the rocket of my life to follow.
I saw the moon a while
in that time of things at pressing work,
it went by very fast.

So, under force of change, or spurt of growth,
everything inside goes backwards, hard,
until it is drawn to steady out –
out, feeling lighter in the all-that-is,
in that new, nothing-happening-seeming
stream of speed.

PETER PORTER

Last Words

In the beginning was the Word,
Not just the Word of God but sounds
Where truth is clarified or blurred.
Then rhyme and rhythm did the rounds
And justified their jumps and joins
By glueing up our lips and groins.

Once words had freshness on their breath.
The poet who saw first that death
Has only one true rhyme was made
The Leader of the Boys' Brigade.
Dead languages can scan and rhyme
Like birthday cards and *Lilac Time*.

And you can carve words on a slab
Or tow them through the air by plane,
Tattoo them with a painful jab
Or hang them in a window pane.
Unlike our bodies which decay,
Words, first and last, have come to stay.

SHEENAGH PUGH

Author, Author

Sunlight and someone I don't know
wrote a smile in your eyes, choreographed
your lightened step, shaped the word 'happy'
between your lips. I hope it outlasts the bright spell,
and though I'd give much to have scripted this,
my thanks to the author.

PETER READING

In Marfa, TX

Zane Grey, the author of Westerns, came to Marfa
a couple of times, researching for his book
The Lone Star Ranger, which he dedicated
to Jeff Vaughan – Ranger, Deputy US Marshal,
Customs Official, Sheriff of Presidio,
served as a judge in the World Series Rodeo
at Madison Square Garden, NY City.
Vaughan had a horse called Jack o' Diamonds, raised
on the Bite Ranch and famous for his style
and custom-crafted saddle with hand carvings
and fancy silver ornamental tooling.

Some feller I met in Ray's Bar told me how
one night, after a dozen or so Lone Stars,
as he was going for home, he saw Jeff Vaughan
on Jack o' Diamonds and Zane Grey on a *burro*
heading down Highland from the County Courthouse.
He mumbled, 'How y'all?' and they said, 'Howdy',
then rode, transparent, plum through the library wall.

PETER REDGROVE

Circus Wheel
(vertical and horizontal)

I

They have driven the Ferris
                out on to the hill
                            powered it with
Its own generators fetched
                out of the tailgate
                            of its painted lorry –
It is like a Christmas tree which
                is a round staircase
                            up to the stars
The planets and their maelstroms
                and among them swing
                            benches for the paying customers
The great wheel declares
                the fair is here
                            And at its foot kiosks cluster
Stuffed with light:
                the fortune-teller's hovel where
                            you put your life-lines
Into her palmist-hands,
                and the dodgems with their
                            high electrical tails
Sparking like meteor-swarms
                hissing on the wire-netting ceiling;
                            all raised up on the muddy green,

Hammered together in one day and one
                    night, it is a piece of
                                star-sky come down
On to the hill and full
                    of folk in this one day
                                the hinge in the year
Where one may peruse
                    star-machinery in close-up
                                raised up on 28 benches
Viewing the mysteries,
                    hanging on the wheel,
                                as in the grand circular tent
Or marquee
                    or tabernacle the horses wheel, gallop
                                each with its mistress
Standing tall
                    and smeared with sequins
                                like glittering
Stallion-stuff.

II

The Wheels of the Fair,
　　　　the outer
　　　　　　　　and the inner as fair,
The outer, the Fairies' Wheel
　　　　　in which the 28 moon-benches
　　　　　　　　　climb to their height
Pulling the reins
　　　　　of the earth's water
　　　　　　　　　like a round harp
And like this equestrienne
　　　　　wearing her khaki
　　　　　　　　　rehearsal-shirt
The colour of earth
　　　　　riding the circus-ring
　　　　　　　　　like a cavalry
She is called Ms O
　　　　　horsed, the ring is her route,
　　　　　　　　　like a Centauress
With mountainous
　　　　　horse-thews
　　　　　　　　　she traces out that
Deep castle of hers,
　　　　　with the dewy pond:
　　　　　　　　　the spinning castle of horseback
And its water is the same
　　　　　glittering stuff
　　　　　　　　　as the estuary water in which

The lights revolve
                that circus which must descend
                        so fair it is,
The Mare-Mother's ring
                the woman's
                        circular fountain,
She rides
        the fairest thing.

DERYN REES JONES

Plums

Home late, I find you asleep,
body turned to the cool moonlight,
an open book on the counterpane,
pale leaves rustling in the breeze.
And everywhere the smell of plums:
an unexpected purple, slipping through
the moth-like curtains, trellising the walls.
There's no note on the bedside table –
just an eyelash on a flushed cheek,
a mouth as sulky as our absent child's.
And no word either, from your dream –
only your lips if I kissed them a clue,
the bed a tree and you its blossom:
delicious, sweet and gold.

CHRISTOPHER REID

Fire-bytes

Once more
hopes soar

burst and scatter
no matter

brief blaze
spent days

*

Shouts of light
against night

bombarded skies
fire eyes

humdrum
days to come

*

Star spill
stay still

brave flare
stop there

in the boundless wow
of now

MAURICE RIORDAN

The Cook's Night Out

the firmament sheweth His handiwork

Nothing much falls from the heavens, not in a day's
                                                 walking
Or the night that follows, out here on the moors:
One shower of hail from the entirely blue, and now
The odd starburst that we think is comet dust
Igniting in the stratosphere – but nothing to match
The skillet-size snowflakes that hit Matt Coleman's ranch
In '32; nothing of signs and wonders,
Neither manna nor the Welshman's *pwdre ser*,
Never mind the parachute fifty years falling on Slough
Or the three suns – the Sun in Splendour! – that shone
On the eve of the Battle at Mortimer's Cross;
And nothing at all to compete with the asteroid-poke,
The lumpy planetesimal plucked from the Main Belt
Or the rugger-ball booted mindlessly out of the Oort Cloud
That knocked the dinosaur off its ledge – not unless we
                                                 start to think
Of the whole shebang taking a breather, a merciful lull,
In which the biochemical soup simmers
On the cosmic hob, while an inconspicuous quadruped,
With opposable thumbs and a nocturnal habit,
Goes on a blinder, leapfrogs from prey to hunter, from
                                                 stalking
To husbandry, as brain and pelvic cavities egg each other on
Towards their tender equilibrium, this steady state

In which our soufflé spirits rise. And nothing falls, nothing
spills.
Or not enough to sizzle the gently smouldering mass
Or collapse the mildly stinging air into a liquid bullet
And cancel one summer's night under the stars.

ROBIN ROBERTSON

*Wedding the Locksmith's Daughter**

The slow-grained slide to embed the blade
of the key is a sheathing,
a gliding on graphite, pushing inside
to find the ribs of the lock.

Sunk home, the true key slots to its matrix;
geared, tight-fitting, they turn
together, shooting the spring-lock,
throwing the bolt. Dactyls, iambics –

the clinch of words – the hidden couplings
in the cased machine. A chime of sound
on sound: the way the sung note snibs on meaning

and holds. The lines engage and marry now
like vows, their bells are keeping time;
the church doors close and open underground.

* locksmith's daughter: nineteenth-century slang for a key

NEIL ROLLINSON

Helpline

I love your calm, unhurried way, that sexy
lilt in your Irish voice as you take me
line by line through the nightmares
of my Autoexec.Bat and Config.Sys files.
We check the registry for clues,
the boot log, BIOS and System.Ini.
It's like love, this language of DOS,
like talking dirty over the phone.
When I tell you it still won't work
you pause for a moment and moan,
like my hands have found the lush peripherals
beneath your anorak.
Well, you say, it seems your system
is corrupt, you'll have to wipe
your hard disk now and reinstall Windows.
I sigh down the phone. Do you want me
to take you through it? You ask.
You could make invalid page faults
and fatal exceptions sound desirable.
I look at your scribbled name on my pad.
Mary, take me gently, I'm yours.

ANNE ROUSE

To the Unknown Lover

We ride through fields of force, with eighteen gears,
down slopes to grace amusement parks,
as a flock of gleaming snow geese wheels
above our wind-blown heads. No one spoke,
ever, until you asked me if I had the time;
and I have the energy, too, my dearest of dumb dears.

I've got the verve of a nanny goat, and a deer's
alertness; I've made my thumbed appraisal of the gears:
'he stops, he looks, he smiles; next time
he'll touch.' On Saturday I clocked you in the park.
I laughed up at the storm-clouds as they spoke.
Let heaven blink its warning as it wills!

I'm subtle as Iago: wheels within wheels
kaleidoscope round your head; 'too dear
for my possessing' – surely not! We spoke,
and now the teeth are rattling on the gears.
A thousand lovers huzzah in the parks.
I haggle with mortality, and time.

Suddenly we meet, it's time.
I stammer and my syntax wheels.
I ask, is it your favourite park?
But watch my eyes: they hold you dear.
This is the bumpiest of gears.
It was easier when we never spoke.

You've put a spoke
in the wheel of time,
and I've put on my evening gear,
so spin the wheel
towards luck (even if it costs me dear).
Let's park.

We park.
A god spoke
to me, dear,
as time
and cosmos wheel
on their stripped gears.

CAROL RUMENS

The Talk Pen

A cool Talk Pen (record and play back your own message),
One litre of ten-year-old Laphroaig, a Re-Vit Body Massage,
A sweater-bear, three hundred grams of Continental Truffles,
A box of Lancôme's *Couleurs*, and assorted cosmetic trifles,
Were found untouched in a duty-free bag in the dead
                                    woman's home
Like chromosomes that had never mated, planes that had
                                    almost flown.

EVA SALZMAN

To the Enemy

Sit down, have a chair and relax,
you who've made former friends bleed.
Here are all my questionable expenses
for the tax-man, the faithless to read.

Okay, so I drink, talk to strangers,
loudly befriending at parties
those lacking position, power or wealth,
who aren't distinguished or arty.

I slept with a man who was handsome
instead of the powerful editor
(not that I've ever claimed purer ethics –
it's just that I never knew better.)

Please outline what's wrong with my life plan,
help map the route of my passions,
edit me into comfortable style
according to science or fashion.

It's not that I don't have ambition
or a liking for money or fame.
Is it just that I misinterpret the rules?
Don't I cheat enough at the game?

PETER SANSOM

Chippie

Don't get me wrong. I believe in change.
Kebab it if you like, batter Mars bars,
but this is my childhood, before
pizza and tandooris, the Balti Cottage
by the Miner's Welfare. I mean
formica counters too high, Tizer,
and England about to win. And yes, I know
nostalgia's not what it was, and it's the same

for our lot, in the lolling queue on Fridays,
then back to unwrap them round the telly;
but sometimes you have to give in
to that still-in-your-school-togs picture,
before spaghetti and quick chill, the burger bar
down from what was the Working Men's,
before anybody's died. A picture
so real, in three dimensions and sudden

it stops you like heart failure or a glass door
or seeing a friend in the Open-All-Day
three o'clock lull and sidling next to him with
'Mek it twice, love, he's paying' —
and of course he's been dead years.
And this bloke, startled, instead of anger
is trying to hide what he can't remember,
handing her a tenner and grinning at you

'How you doing?' (The sizzling splash
of a bucket of raw chips.) So you smile, too,
you can't complain. Two grown men, stood there
while she shovels another portion
and lays another giant haddock on,
then steps back for both of you to lean
and season them at the same time.
'It must be ages,' he says. And you agree.

WILLIAM SCAMMELL

Blue

Kippered in cigarette smoke
and needled with marginalia
my first editions won't be worth much
to my heirs, nor the letters and biographies,
the tasteful pictures, the one-off brass
musician and stone goddess
of doubtful provenance and mythological
sex appeal, bought somewhere east
of Tunis on a windy Thursday
when the Med churned up heaps
of seaweed on a ploughed, empty beach
three-quarters clean again next day.

That was then. Now the big logs outside
stick together, cauterized by frost,
as though one sawing was enough.
It seems cruel to tread on the icy grass.
Blade cold and sunny under a high
blue dome, the vaunted crystal firmament.
This is how it was in the old days
before we cooked it up into rain.

Here's a blackbird scuttling in
on his broomstick, quick as a flash,
quicker than his own startled call.

And here's you in the old raincoat
down to your ankles, that witching hair,
come to see what marriage looks like
in the open air.

PENELOPE SHUTTLE

Scholar's Shop

He has farewells
like jewels,
he has thoughts like a tree
of thoughts,
or like little crusts of bread,
he has books of a calmness
not to be found anywhere else. Yet
he is as a false jewel
to himself, a sky unfolded without thought.
He has continuance,
like the sun or the moon.
He has Venice and Genoa
for shield and protection. He has hope
in the form of a globe. He has storms,
like riches. He assembles in crowds,
in leapyear biographies. He washes over me
in faiths of water, frosts of light,
cloud-memoirs. He shows me
how to design a peach, how to find
a landscape not yet two years old,
he is progressive as a comet,
sparkling, icy, all tail and purpose,
or wears his bird mask
to build an aviary by the sea.
He has farewells like patience,
like all the world's colours appearing before their judge.

KEN SMITH

Near Barking

The state I'm in, another fugue somewhere
south of north, not far off by the sexagesimal reckoning,
though all that is just another pair of trousers
in another order of events, and this where I am now
is already the other side of that. Here is where I'll be,
living near Barking wherever Barking is, at midnight
on the moment as the arbitrary settings of time
tip us out with a bad hangover into the next thousand years,
a device designed to get us to forget ourselves again,
waking in a new dawn with a new minted identity.

In the last words of the sailor king *bugger Bognor,*
let me die in bloody peace. Are you sure it's safe?
the last utterance of Will Palmer, hanged for murder
in 1856. *On the whole I'd rather be in Philadelphia.*
It's true much of the time it is very boring,
sitting in some place nursing a gursache
so yes I'll have another drink and think
of all the pretty bottles behind the bar
I'll never taste, all the bars in all the world
I'll never visit, all the blue skies, all the women.
You know it's funny how you forget heatwaves,
and what was the name of that distant country
of which we knew little, whatever went on there
is a fictionalised account by now, the answer
to all these dusty answers is just dusty.

So let the last night begin, in the deepening blue
the blackbird and the evening star, the other stars
winking on, their messages across the distances say
here, I'm here, still here, out here, over here
in all this enormity, that is to say nowhere
in particular, this speck among the tides of the vast dust
spread out across the time it makes up as it travels.
Whether the machines cease or no on the midnight
I'll be here, no doubt as usual engaged
in my inconclusive experiment with alcohol,
speculating this red ten takes that black jack,
this black pawn that white bishop, muttering
aloud these words I've made to be the last words
delivered at the last minute, ending in a dream of flying.

PAULINE STAINER

The Snake-dancer

is surrounded by a circle of ice,
glass-snakes coiled
on her head.

They pour down and sway,
mapping the warmth
of her body.

But that whisper – is it just
their skulls of fluid bone
grazing the ice

or *the desire of the line*,
melting, insatiable,
as the ice floats the sun?

ANNE STEVENSON

A Ballad for Apothecaries

Being a Poem to Honour the Memory of
Nicholas Culpeper, Gent.,
Radical, Apothecary, Herbalist, Astrologer,
Who in the Year of our Lord 1649
Did publish *A Physical Directory*
Translated from the Latin of the London Dispensatory made by
the College of Physicians
'Being that Book by which all Apothecaries are strictly
commanded to make all their Physicke.'

In sixteen-hundred-and-sixteen
(The year Will Shakespeare died),
The earth made a pact with a curious star,
And a new-born baby cried.

Queen Bess's bright spring was over.
James Stuart frowned from the throne.
A more turbulent, seditious people
England had never known.

Now, Nick was a winsome baby,
And Nick was a lively lad.
They gowned him and sent him to Cambridge
Where he went, said the priests, to the bad.

For although he excelled in Latin
And could rattle the Gospels in Greek,
Nick thought to himself, there's more to be said
Than the Ancients knew how to speak.

He was led to alchemical study
Through a deep Paracelsian text;
He took up the art of astrology first,
The science of botany next.

To the theories of Galen he listened,
To those of Hippocrates, too.
But he said to himself, there is more to be done
Than the Ancients knew how to do.

For though Dr Tradition's a rich man,
He charges a rich man's fee.
Dr Reason and Dr Experience
Are my guides in philosophy.

The College of Learned Physicians
Prescribes for the ruling class:
Physick for the ills of the great, they sneer,
Won't do for the vulgar mass.

But I say the heart of a beggar
Is as good as the heart of a king,
And the English blood in our English veins
Is of equal valuing.

Poor Nick fell in love with an heiress,
But en route to their desperate tryst,
The lady was struck down by lightning
Before they'd embraced or kissed.

So our hero consulted the Heavens
Where he saw he was fated to be
Friend to the sick and the humble
But the Grand World's enemy.

Nick packed up his books in Cambridge,
And went down without a degree
To inspirit Red Lion Street, Spitalfields,
With fiery humanity.

As a reckless, unlicensed physician,
He was moved to disseminate
Cures for the ills of the body
With cures for the ills of the state.

Who knows what horrors would have happened
To Nicholas Culpeper, Gent.,
If the king hadn't driven his kingdom
Into war with Parliament!

In the ranks of the New Model Army
Nick fought with the medical men,
Till a Royalist bullet at Newbury
Shot him back to his thundering pen.

'Scholars are the people's jailors,
And Latin's their jail,' he roared,
'Our fates are in thrall to knowledge;
Vile men would have knowledge obscured!'

When they struck King Charles's head off
Nick Culpeper cried, 'Amen.'
O it's well that he died before the day
They stuck it on again.

Still, English tongues won their freedom
In those turbulent years set apart;
And the wise still cherish Nick's courage
While they cheer his compassionate heart.

So whenever you stop in a chemist's
For an aspirin or salve for a sore,
Give a thought to Nicholas Culpeper
Who dispensed to the London poor.

For cures for the ills of the body
Are cures for the ills of the mind;
And a welfare state is a sick state
If the dumb are led by the blind.

Note:

In a series of prefaces to his best-selling *A Physical Directory* (1649, reprinted at least fourteen times before 1718) Culpeper denounced the College of Physicians who secured their monopoly by keeping the secrets of medicine in the Latin language. 'A company of proud insulting, domineering doctors, whose wits were born above 500 years before themselves,' he called them. This translation of the *Pharmacopoeia Londinensis* was made, he wrote, 'out of pure pity to the commonality of England . . . many of whom to my knowledge have perished either for want of money to fee a physician or want of knowledge of a remedy happily growing in their garden.'

Culpeper's translation of the *Pharmacopoeia*, together with a *Directory for Midwives* and others of his seventy-nine books and pamphlets, sold in huge numbers. In 1652–3 he brought out at least two editions of his celebrated herbal under the title *The English Physitian: or, an Astrological–Physical Discourse of the Vulgar Herbs of this Nation, Being a Compleat Method of Physick, whereby a man may preserve his Body in Health, or cure himself, being sick, for three pence charge, with such things as grow in England, they being most fit for English Bodies.*

Though Culpeper was accused by his enemies of being a charlatan (and I believe no pharmacist would recommend an uncritical recourse to Culpeper's remedies today), his *Physical Directory* remained in print into the eighteenth century and his celebrated herbal continues to be influential even today. Sadly, Culpeper, for all his medical knowledge, was not able to prevent his own death, aged thirty-eight, in 1654, nor the deaths of six of his seven children who predeceased him.

I am indebted to *The Dictionary of National Biography; Culpeper's Complete Herbal*, (Hereford: Wordsworth Editions, 1995); Graeme Tobyn's *Culpeper's Medicine*, (USA, 1997); Christopher Hill's *Intellectual Origins of the English Revolution*, (Oxford, 1965); and to *A Winter Herbal, plucked from the pages of Nicholas Culpeper, Gent.*, a pamphlet privately printed by Jill Paton Walsh and John Rowe Townsend in December, 1998.

MATTHEW SWEENEY

A Smell of Fish

A smell of fish filled the valley
and all the seagulls came inland.

Cats ran everywhere, sniffing.
Men checked the level of the sea.

Some could be heard hammering.
Churches filled to pray for wind.

GEORGE SZIRTES

Flash

When she looked through the view-finder she found
him changed. It was the shadow of a moment
that made the difference, one in a vast torrent
of light that seemed to have lifted her from the ground,
Perhaps the bomb had finally fallen. He
was still smiling but had dropped through a trapdoor
on the other side of the world. No more
time was left, it was all eternity.

Then she pressed the shutter and it went click
as it always does, and there he was, smiling
but elsewhere. Elsewhere was where they both were.
And it was green, attractive, beguiling
as they returned, the earth steady and pure,
washed clean, as if by hypo or by magic.

CHARLES TOMLINSON

Ode to Memory

'Bird-witted'
is unjust –
call them all
winged memories: food
stowed and stored
to them means
food to be recalled:
they can trace months later
the where and when,
and what we would leave
forgotten, they will retrieve
in order of preference,
i.e., that which tastes best,
or should, if rot
has not decayed it: respect
the despised intellect
of birds, and when a name
out of the hundred that you know
refuses to appear
wish yourself bird-gifted,
and then go airily outside,
and on lifted wings
re-train the sights
of unfocused recollection, and if you can
become bird-brained.

SUSAN WICKS

Optician

His pencil of light
draws me the bare branches
of my eye's blood,
sap rising in darkness
deep under the lid.

A frieze of trees repeating
on my wall of red –
the shades I lost,
painted by touch,
blaze under his torch.

Now the light is out
but the lines wait –
my deer and bison running
in their red cave.
The fire they outlive.

JOHN HARTLEY WILLIAMS

How the First Kite was Flown

A kite is simply a pen, I thought,
dipped in the ink of heaven.
We went up the hill for the wind
to read what it might send.

Planted there, I held the line
& traced the ideograms
of its pelican nose-dives,
its loopy swoops and curves.

Two girls, with eager faces,
their mother in silken green –
a dragon around her waist –
followed the feints of my wrist.

I, mandarin, master of pigtails,
fierce behind my cuneiform mustache,
inscribed upon the sky
a text to make them smile.

The levity of their delight
at what I did with gravity
was good to see: my scribbling
on the airy blue of nothing.

HUGO WILLIAMS

Slapstick

(Joseph Grimaldi 1781–1837)

No sooner born than bouncing off the walls
of Sadler's Wells,
whirled round the head of his father,
an Italian dentist turned ballet master,
'not a very good clown',
constantly falling down,
drunken, syphilitic, incestuous,
unable to express himself
without violence or sex,
till one day the chain breaks
and Little Joey Grimaldi
– Robinson Crusoe's faithful monkey –
goes flying away from his father
into the arms of a spectator.

Grimaldi Senior's low comedy Clown
is too much, even for his son,
who finds he has a flare
for parental caricature,
dressing up and spouting nonsense at everyone
in cod Italian.
'I am Grim-all-day,' he tells his hangers-on,
'but I make you laugh at night.'
When the old man catches the little mite
making fun of him backstage,
he beats him without mercy,

puts him in the monkey's cage
and hoists him into the flies
to cool off, an act which induces
his own death from apoplexy.

Now it is up to Little Joey
to put aside childish bruises
and step into his father's shoes
as himself, whoever that may be.
He will soon be recognisable
as 'Senior Guzzle',
swigging from a whisky bottle,
swaggering about the stage
gobbling strings of sausages,
trays of jam tarts with lashings
of whipped cream on top,
dishing out slapstick thrashings
to anyone who tries to stop him,
falling down and being arrested.

He'll come on as Sir Feeble Sordid
in a post-chaise made from a basket
and two cheeses, his coat encrusted
with frills and spots in the manner
of his failed dandy father.
In coal scuttle 'boots' and candlestick 'spurs'
he drills officers
of a swell cavalry regiment
with such an air of hauteur
that a note of protest is sent
to the Manager,
threatening withdrawal of the Royal Warrant.
In a duel 'to the death'

he and his opponent
shoot their seconds with blunderbusses
and shake hands over the corpses.

In mid-life, spasms and cramps
affect his performance.
Every bone in his body has been broken
at least once
in the countless comic kickings
and pratfalls he has undertaken
in the name of comedy.
'I am Grim-all-day,' he tells his audience,
'so why do you laugh at me?'
In pain, reduced to performing in a chair,
he consults a doctor,
who takes one look at his gloomy countenance
and refers him elsewhere:
'There is only one thing for you, sir.
You must go and see Grimaldi the Clown.'

His days of laughter long gone,
Grimaldi passes on
the rudiments of his profession
to his son Young Joe,
who does his best to follow
his father's patient tuition,
swigging from a bottle of whisky,
falling down too often,
making a mockery
of the delicate art of slapstick.
He'll go on frantic
pickpocketing sprees through the audience,
do a dance with a lobster,

but fail to get a laugh
without his father's genial bluster
to carry it all off.

Now Young Joe descends
into real-life debauchery,
drinking too much, getting into fights,
falling down unconscious
and not coming home at night,
a way of life which ends
with breakdown and death
at the age of thirty-one,
his fate a natural extension
of his father's greatest creation
of Guzzle the Clown,
known and loved throughout the city
for making mock of authority,
stuffing himself with junk food,
falling down drunk.

Depressed by the death of his son
and that of his second wife Mary Bristow,
Grimaldi lingers like a ghost
in the ingle-nook
of his local hostelry,
The Marquis of Cornwallis,
carried home each night
on the back of the landlord William Cook,
to his lodgings in Southampton Street,
where only his beloved breeding pigeons
flutter a welcome.

'God bless you, my son,' he tells the young man
as the faithful publican
lays him down in the candlelight.
'I shall be ready for you tomorrow night.'

GERARD WOODWARD

Giant

Six months in the north
And I have burgled the dolls' house,
My hands through the windows
Like a scientist handling
Uranium gloved, through a wall,
     But my fingers still burn

When I think of them filling
Those little rooms. Midnight
And they were still awake.
I can't sleep for what I've done.
My prints big as rugs
     On those untrodden floors.

I could go south again,
Back to the ordinary houses.
It was when I unhasped the frontage
And found it opened like a book
That I nearly fainted,
     Rooms dissected, an exploded view

Of unwanted intimacy,
Those blindly alert faces.
The sadness of my heist
Hit me when I emptied
My pockets, for they contained
     Absurdities – a pill-sized

Light bulb, chairs upholstered
In moleskin that wouldn't seat
A rat, chandeliers like earrings,
A fingernail diadem. I can't
Return them. The whole house
    Slammed shut. I ran.

I stayed two months
With my wife and family. My eldest
Uncle, John, left me an estate
In land near Epping. I set my cattle
Down and left them to graze
    On a bowling green in Greenwich.

KIT WRIGHT

Fireworks Poems

(i) A Comfort in Grey & Purple & Gold

If you die of misery one of these grey afternoons,
If you die of horror one of these purple nights,
there is always the golden advance consolation:
THIS DOES NOT AFFECT YOUR STATUTORY RIGHTS!

(ii) Honesty

So pure and still a purple
breathing at dusk from the tall mantles
ruined into paper coins
and helpless see-through tears of honesty . . .

The Poets

Dannie Abse's most recent volume of poems was *Arcadia, One Mile* (1998). He has also published a selection from his previous books, *Welsh Retrospective*.

Fleur Adcock was born in Auckland, New Zealand. She studied Classics at Wellington University, and moved to London in 1963. *Selected Poems* (1991) represents six earlier volumes; her most recent collection is *Looking Back* (1997). She has also edited the *Faber Book of Twentieth Century Women's Poetry*.

Fred D'Aguiar was born in London and brought up in Guyana and London. He has written poetry, fiction and for the theatre and television. His book-length narrative poem *Bill of Rights* was shortlisted for the 1998 T. S. Eliot Prize. He teaches English at the University of Miami.

Simon Armitage was born in 1963 and lives in Huddersfield. He has published seven books of poetry, as well as a prose memoir, and has written extensively for radio and television. He teaches in this country and in America. His plays include a version of Euripides' *Heracles*.

Peter Armstrong was born in Blaydon-on-Tyne in 1957. His collections are *Risings* and *The Red-Funnelled Boat*.

Sujata Bhatt was born in Ahmedabad, India, in 1956. She was educated in the US and now lives in Bremen with her husband, the German writer Michael Augustin, and their daughter. She has been the recipient of the Commonwealth Poetry Prize and a Cholmondeley Award in 1991. Her recent books include *The Stinking Rose* and *Selected Poems: Point No Point*.

Charles Boyle lives in London. His last collection was *Paleface* (1996).

Alan Brownjohn is the author of nine books of poems, the most recent of which is *In the Cruel Arcade*. With his wife, Sandy Brownjohn, he has edited three teaching anthologies for secondary schools. He has also translated Goethe's *Torquato Tasso* and Corneille's *Horace*, which was staged at the Lyric Theatre in 1996.

John Burnside is the author of six books of poems, the most recent of which was *A Normal Skin* (1997). He received the Geoffrey Faber Prize in 1994 for *Feast Days*. His novels include *The Dumb House* and *The Mercy Boys*.

Charles Causley has lived all his life in Launceston in Cornwall, where he worked for many years as a teacher. In 1967, he received the Queen's Gold Medal for Poetry and was appointed CBE in 1986. Two recent publications are *Collected Poems for Children* and *Collected Poems 1951–1997*.

Kate Clanchy was born in Glasgow in 1965. *Slattern* (1996) won a number of literary awards including the Somerset Maugham Award and the Forward Prize for Best First Collection. *Samarkand* appeared in 1999.

David Constantine's most recent collection was *The Pelt of Wasps* (1998). He is presently at work on translations of Hölderlin's *Oedipus* and *Antigone*, and a biography of Sir William Hamilton.

Wendy Cope was an inner-city teacher until the publication of her first book of poems, *Making Cocoa for Kingsley Amis*. Her second collection, *Serious Concerns*, has sold more than 85,000 copies. She has also written poems for children and edited four anthologies. In 1987 she won the Cholmondeley Award and in 1995 the American Academy of Arts and Letters Michael Braude Award.

Robert Crawford's collections of poetry include *A Scottish Assembly, Talkies, Masculinity, Spirit Machines*, and in Scots, *Sharawaggi* (with W. N. Herbert). With Simon Armitage he co edited the *Penguin Book of Poetry from Britain and Ireland Since 1945*. He is Professor of Modern Scottish Literature at the University of St Andrews.

David Dabydeen was born in Guyana and educated there and at Cambridge. He has published three books of poems and four novels, the latest of which is *A Harlot's Progress*. He was awarded the Commonwealth Poetry Prize for his first collection, *Slave Song*. He presently teaches at the University of Warwick.

Amanda Dalton was born in Coventry in 1957. Her narrative sequence *Room of Leaves* was recently dramatized for broadcast on Radio 4. She has won prizes in several major poetry competitions, and her first full-length collection, *How To Disappear*, was published in 1999.

Peter Didsbury has published three full-length collections: *The Butchers of Hull, The Classical Farm* and *That Old-Time Religion*. His second and third books were Poetry Book Society recommendations. He received the Cholmondeley Award in 1989. He works as an archaeological consultant in Hull.

Michael Donaghy was born in the Bronx, New York, in 1954 and studied at the University of Chicago, where he was poetry editor of the *Chicago Review*. He moved to Britain in 1985 and lives in North London. His collections are *Shibboleth*, which won the Whitbread and Geoffrey Faber prizes, and *Errata*, which received awards from the Arts Council of England and the Ingram Merrill Foundation. He is a Fellow of the Royal Society of Literature.

Maura Dooley's collections, *Explaining Magnetism* and *Kissing a Bone*, and her anthology, *Making for Planet Alice*, were all Poetry Book Society recommendations. She was given an Eric Gregory Award, and has been shortlisted for the T. S. Eliot Prize. She has also edited *How Novelists Work*, and is currently preparing a new anthology, *The Honey Gatherers: Love Poetry*, as well as a book on film-making.

Carol Ann Duffy has published several collections of poetry. Her new collection, *The World's Wife*, was published in 1999. A book of poems for children, *Meeting Midnight*, and a book for young readers, *Rumpelstiltskin and Other Grimm Tales*, are currently in preparation.

Ian Duhig was one of the 'New Generation' poets and has won the Northern and the National Poetry competitions. He has held creative writing fellowships at Leeds and Lancaster universities, and his most recent book is *Nominies* (1998).

Helen Dunmore is a poet, novelist and short story writer. Her latest poetry collection is *Bestiary* (1997) and her most recent novel *Your Blue-Eyed Boy* (1998).

Douglas Dunn was born in Renfrewshire, and worked as a librarian before reading English at Hull University. He is Professor of English and founding Head of the School of Scottish Studies at St Andrews University. *Elegies* (1985) won the Whitbread Prize. His most recent collection is *Dante's Drumkit* (1993).

U. A. Fanthorpe has had three careers so far: teacher, hospital receptionist and poet. She has published six collections of poetry and a *Selected Poems*. Her most recent publications are the book *Safe As Houses* and the audiobook *Double Act* (with R. V. Bailey).

Paul Farley's *The Boy from the Chemist is Here to See You* won the 1998 Forward Prize for the Best First Collection. He has also received a Somerset Maugham Award, and in 1999, was named Sunday Times Young Writer of the Year.

Vicki Feaver's collection of poems, *The Handless Maiden*, was awarded a Heinemann Prize and shortlisted for the Forward Prize. A selection of her poems is also included in *Penguin Modern Poets 2*.

Roy Fisher was born in 1930 in Birmingham. Writer and jazz musician, he lives in Earl Sterndale, Derbyshire. Much of his earlier work, from *City* (1961) onward, is included in *The Dow Low Drop: New and Selected Poems* (1996).

John Glenday was born in Dundee in 1952. *The Apple Ghost* received an SAC Book Award and *Undark* was a Poetry Book Society recommendation for 1995. In 1990, he was the Scottish Canadian Exchange Fellow based at the University of Alberta. He currently works as a drugs counsellor in Dundee.

Lavinia Greenlaw was born in London in 1962. Her books are *Night Photograph* (1993) and *A World Where News Travelled Slowly* (1997).

Andrew Greig was born in Bannockburn in 1951. He now lives in Orkney and the Lothians. He is the author of five collections of poems, two mountaineering books and three novels, the most recent of which is *When They Lay Bare* (1999).

Sophie Hannah is currently a Fellow Commoner in Creative Arts at Trinity College, Cambridge. She has published three collections of poems: *The Hero and the Girl Next Door*, *Hotels Like Houses* and *Leaving and Leaving You*, as well as a novel, *Gripless*.

David Harsent has published seven collections of poems. His *Selected Poems* appeared in 1989. He has collaborated with Harrison Birtwistle on the opera *Gawain* and the song cycle *The Woman and The Hare*. In 1997 he published *Sprinting From the Graveyard*, English versions of poems by the Bosnian, Goran Simic. His most recent book was *A Bird's Idea of Flight*, which was shortlisted for the T. S. Eliot Prize.

W. N. Herbert was born in Dundee in 1961. He read English at Oxford, and currently lives in Newcastle. Among his collections in English and Scots are *Sharawaggi* (with Robert Crawford, 1990), *Cabaret McGonagall* (1996) and the *Laurelude* (1998). He is also author of the critical study *To Circumjack McDiarmid* (1992).

Tracey Herd is currently writer in residence at Dundee University. *No Hiding Place* (1996) was shortlisted for the Forward Prize for Best First Collection. A selection of new work appears in the anthology *New Blood* (1999).

Selima Hill is currently working on an opera with the Danish composer Bent Sorensen; on an anthology of dog poems; and on a seventh collection, *Bunny*. She has won both the Cholmondeley Award and the Arvon/Observer Poetry Competition. *Violet* was nominated for the Forward, T. S. Eliot and Whitbread prizes in 1998/9.

Tobias Hill lives in London. He has been the recipient of

numerous literary awards; his collections are *Midnight in the City of Clocks* (1996) and *Zoo* (1998). *Skin*, a volume of short stories, won the PEN/Macmillan Prize for fiction.

Michael Hofmann was born in Freiburg and grew up in England and the United States. He studied English at Cambridge. Since 1983 he has worked as a reviewer and translator from German. Recent collections include *Acrimony* (1986) and *Corona Corona* (1993). With James Lasdun, he edited *After Ovid: New Metamorphoses*.

Mick Imlah was born in 1956 in Aberdeen and was educated at Oxford. He is the author of *Birthmarks* (1989) and co-editor of the new *Penguin Book of Scottish Verse*.

Kathleen Jamie's books include *The Queen of Sheba* (1994) and *Jizzen* (1999). She has won several awards for her work, including the Somerset Maugham and Geoffrey Faber awards.

Alan Jenkins was born in 1955, lives in London and has been deputy editor of the *TLS* since 1990. His last book, *Harm*, won the 1994 Forward Prize.

Jackie Kay has written poetry for adults and children. Her latest collection, *Off Colour* (1998), was shortlisted for the T. S. Eliot Prize. Her first novel, *Trumpet* (1998), won the Guardian Fiction Prize.

Mimi Khalvati was born in Iran in 1944. She has published three collections: *In White Ink, Mirrorwork* and *Entries on Light*. She is co-ordinator of the Poetry School in London.

Tom Leonard was born in 1944 in Glasgow. His gathered poetry 1964–83, *Intimate Voices*, shared the Scottish Book of the Year award in 1984. A further selection from 1984–94 was

Reports from the Present. He has also published *Places in the Mind*, a biography of the Scottish poet James Thomson, and compiled *Radical Renfrew Poetry: From the French Revolution to the First World War.*

Michael Longley was born in 1939, and educated at the Royal Belfast Academical Institution, and Trinity College, Dublin. He is married to the critic Edna Longley. A new *Selected Poems* appeared in 1998.

Roddy Lumsden was born in St Andrews in 1966. He currently lives in London. He received an Eric Gregory Award in 1991, and was Writing Fellow for the City of Aberdeen from 1995–6. His first collection, *Yeah Yeah Yeah*, was shortlisted for a Forward Prize.

Sarah Maguire has published two collections of poetry: *Spilt Milk* and *The Invisible Mender*. She is currently editing *Flora Poetica: The Chatto Book of Botanical Verse.*

Glyn Maxwell was born in 1962 in Welwyn Garden City. His first book of poems, *Tale of the Mayor's Son* (1990), was a Poetry Book Society choice. *Out of the Rain* followed in 1992, winning the Somerset Maugham Award, and *Rest for the Wicked* in 1995. He has also written a novel, *Blue Burneau*, a number of verse plays and is currently adapting Malory's *Morte D'Arthur* for the Royal Shakespeare Company. He is Visiting Writer at Amherst College, Massachusetts.

Roger McGough was born in Liverpool and now lives in London. He has won the Cholmondeley Award, and has received an OBE. His latest collection is *The Ways Things Are.*

Medbh McGuckian is a Belfast poet and has recently received the Irish American Literary Award and the Denis Devlin Prize for Poetry.

Jamie McKendrick was born in Liverpool, and has published three books of poetry: *The Sirocco Room, The Kiosk on the Brink*, and *The Marble Fly* – the last a Poetry Book Society choice and winner of the Forward Prize.

Paula Meehan is an award-winning Irish poet and playwright who lives and works in Dublin. A selection of her poetry has been published as *Mysteries of the Home*.

Adrian Mitchell was born in the 30s, educated by wolves and elephants in the 40s, raged in the 50s, raved publicly in the 60s, staged plays for adults in the 70s, and plays for adults and children in the 80s and 90s. His recent books include *Blue Coffee* and *Heart on the Left*.

Edwin Morgan was born in Glasgow in 1920. He retired as Titular Professor of English at Glasgow University in 1980. His books include *Selected Poems* (1985), *Collected Poems* (1990), *Sweeping Out the Dark, Virtual and Other Realities*, and a translation of Rostand's *Cyrano de Bergerac* into Scots. The last-named won the Stakis Prize for Scottish Writer of the Year in 1998.

Blake Morrison was born in Skipton, Yorkshire, in 1950. He was formerly the literary editor of the *Independent on Sunday*. His prose memoir *And When Did You Last See Your Father?* was the winner of the 1993 Esquire/Volvo/Waterstone's Non-Fiction Award and the J. R. Ackerley Prize for Autobiography. *Too True*, a collection of his stories and journalism, was published in 1998.

Andrew Motion was born in 1952. His books include *The*

Pleasure Steamers, Secret Narratives and *Love in a Life*. His awards include the John Llewelyn Rhys Memorial Prize and the Arvon/Observer Prize. In 1999 he was invested as Poet Laureate.

Paul Muldoon has recently been appointed as the Oxford Professor of Poetry. He is Howard G. B. Clark Professor of the Humanities and Creative Writing at Princeton University, and President of the Poetry Society. His most recent collection is *Hay* (1998).

Eiléan Ní Chuilleanáin was born in 1942, and teaches at Trinity College, Dublin. She is married to the poet Macdara Woods, and they have one son, Niall. Her recent books include *The Second Voyage* and *The Brazen Serpent*.

Grace Nichols was born in Guyana but has lived in Britain since 1977. Her first book of poems, *I is a Long-Memoried Woman*, won the 1983 Commonwealth Poetry Prize. Her other collections include *The Fat Black Woman's Poems* and *Lazy Thoughts of a Lazy Woman*. Her latest is a collection of children's poems, *Asana and the Animals*. She has also published a novel, *Whole of a Morning Sky*.

Sean O'Brien's last book of poems, *Ghost Train*, won the Forward Prize. He edited the anthology *The Firebox: Poetry in Britain and Ireland After 1945* (1998) and has written a book of essays on contemporary poetry, *The Deregulated Muse* (1998).

Bernard O'Donoghue's most recent book of poems is *Here Nor There* (1999). He has also edited *Oxford Irish Quotations* (1999). His third collection, *Gunpowder*, won the Whitbread Poetry Prize.

Ruth Padel writes the 'Sunday Poem' discussion column for the *Independent on Sunday*. She won the 1996 National Poetry

Competition, and has published four collections; *Angel* was a Poetry Book Society recommendation, and *Rembrandt Would Have Loved You* was a Poetry Book Society choice, and also shortlisted for the 1998 T. S. Eliot Prize. She is currently at work on a prose study of maleness, rock music and Greek myth.

Tom Paulin's new collection of poems, *The Wind Dog*, was published in 1999.

Katherine Pierpoint is the author of *Truffle Beds* (1995), which was shortlisted for the T. S. Eliot Prize. In 1996, she won a Somerset Maugham Award and was named Sunday Times Young Writer of the Year.

Peter Porter was born in Brisbane in 1929. His *Collected Poems 1961–1999* were published for his seventieth birthday in 1999. Poet, journalist and broadcaster, he has received the Duff Cooper Prize, Whitbread Poetry Prize and the Gold Medal of the Australian Society of Literature. He lives in Central London.

Sheenagh Pugh was born in 1950, lives in Cardiff and teaches at the University of Glamorgan. Her latest collection is *Stonelight*. She won the Forward Prize for Best Individual Poem in 1998, and the Cholmondeley Award in 1999.

Peter Reading has published eighteen books, gathered together in *Collected Poems* in two volumes (1985 & 1986). His two most recent collections are *Work in Regress* and *Ob*.

Peter Redgrove lives in Cornwall with his wife, Penelope Shuttle. His most recent books are *Assembling a Ghost* and *Orchard End*; a new *Selected Poems* appeared in 1999. With Penelope Shuttle, he co-authored their book on menstrual poetics, *The Wise Wound*. He was awarded the Queen's Gold Medal for Poetry in 1996.

Deryn Rees Jones currently co-ordinates the new Reading and Writing Poetry MA at Liverpool Hope University. Her first collection, *The Memory Tray* (1994), was shortlisted for a Forward Prize. In 1996, she received an Arts Council Writer's Award. Her most recent collection is *Signs Round a Dead Body*.

Christopher Reid was poetry editor at Faber from 1991 to 1999. His most recent collection was *Expanded Universes* (1996).

Maurice Riordan was born in Lisgoold, County Clare, in 1953. *A Word from the Loki* was a Poetry Book Society choice. He presently lives in London.

Robin Robertson is from the north-east coast of Scotland. *A Painted Field* won the Forward Prize for Best First Collection, the Aldeburgh Poetry Festival Prize and the Saltire Society Award. His poetry has appeared in a number of anthologies including *Penguin Modern Poets 13*.

Neil Rollinson was born in Yorkshire and studied Fine Art at Newcastle before taking up writing full time. His first book, *A Spillage of Mercury*, was published in 1996, and in 1997 he won first prize in the National Poetry Competition.

Anne Rouse was raised in Virginia and has lived in London since 1974. She has worked for the NHS and the mental health charity MIND. Her two collections are *Sunset Grill* and *Timing*, both Poetry Book Society recommendations. She was a selected poet at the Poetry Café, Covent Garden, for the summer of 1998.

Carol Rumens currently divides her time between England and Northern Ireland where she teaches creative writing at Queen's University, Belfast. Her latest collection of poems is *Holding Pattern*, which has been nominated for a Belfast City Arts Award. She edits an occasional literary magazine, *Brangle*.

Eva Salzman was born in 1960 in New York and grew up in Brooklyn. She has worked as a dancer and bookseller. Her collections are *The English Earthquake* and *Bargain With the Watchman*, both of which received Poetry Book Society recommendations.

Peter Sansom's third collection will be *Point of Sale* – based partly on his Poetry Society Marks and Spencer residency. He has published *Writing Poems*, and is director of the Poetry Business in Huddersfield.

William Scammell won the National Poetry Competition in 1989 and received a Cholmondeley Award for his first book, *Yes and No* (1979). He has published a further eight collections, most recently *All Set to Fall Off the Edge of the World* (1998). He has also written a critical study of Keith Douglas, and edited Ted Hughes' prose essays, *Winter Pollen*.

Penelope Shuttle lives in Cornwall with her husband Peter Redgrove and daughter Zoe. Her *Selected Poems 1980–1996* appeared in 1998, and was a Poetry Book Society recommendation. She is currently working on a new collection, *A Leaf Out of His Book*. She is also co-author (with Peter Redgrove) of *The Wise Wound*.

Ken Smith has published several collections, the most recent of them *Wild Root*. He also received the Lannan Award in 1977, and a Cholmondeley Award in 1998.

Pauline Stainer has published four collections of poetry. *The Honeycomb, Sighting the Slave-Ship* and *The Ice-Pilot Speaks* were Poetry Book Society recommendations. Her last collection, *The Wound-Dresser's Dream*, was shortlisted for the Whitbread Prize. She lives in Rousay in the Orkney Islands.

Anne Stevenson's *Collected Poems 1955–1995* appeared in 1996. Her prose works include *Bitter Fame – A Life of Sylvia Plath, Five Looks at Elizabeth Bishop, Between the Iceberg and the Ship*, and *Selected Essays*. She received the Athena Award in 1990.

Matthew Sweeney's most recent publications are *Cacti* and *The Bridal Suite*. He is also the co-author of *Writing Poetry* and a selection of his work was included in *Penguin Modern Poets 12*. He was the recipient of an Arts Council Writer's Award in 1999.

George Szirtes' *Selected Poems* appeared in 1996, and *Portrait of My Father in an English Landscape* in 1998. He has won both Geoffrey Faber and Cholmondeley Awards, and has been shortlisted for the Whitbread Prize. He is also a prize-winning translator, a broadcaster and children's poet.

Charles Tomlinson was born in Stoke on Trent, and now lives in Gloucestershire, having taught at Bristol University for thirty-six years. His *Selected Poems 1955–1997* appeared in 1997. He has been the recipient of both the Bennet Award for Poetry and the Cittadella European Prize.

Susan Wicks is the author of three collections of poetry, the most recent of which is *The Clever Daughter* (1997). Her first, *Singing Underwater*, won the Aldeburgh Poetry Festival Prize, and her second, *Open Diagnosis*, was one of the Poetry Society's 'New Generation' titles. She has also published a short memoir, *Driving My Father*, and two novels.

John Hartley Williams' recent publications include *Ignoble, Sentiments* (1995), and *Canada* (1997), which was a Poetry Book Society choice, and shortlisted for the T. S. Eliot Prize.

His translations from the Serbo-Croat, *The Scar in the Stone*, appeared in 1998.

Hugo Williams was born in 1942, worked as a editorial assistant on the *London* magazine, then as a freelance theatre, film and television critic. His American travels are recorded in *No Particular Place to Go*, and his *TLS* columns collected in *Freelancing*. His poetry books include *Writing Home* and *Dock Leaves*, both Poetry Book Society choices.

Gerard Woodward's third collection, *Island to Island*, was published in 1999. He lives in Manchester where he works as a freelance artist.

Kit Wright is a freelance poet, children's author, short story writer and broadcaster. His last book of poems for adults was *Short Afternoons*, which won the Hawthornden Prize and the Heinemann Prize for Poetry. He lives in East London.

Index of Poets, Titles, Places and Events*

Poems shown in an exhibition at Salisbury Arts Centre

Helen Dunmore – *Ice Coming*
U. A. Fanthorpe – *Words for Months*
Roy Fisher – *And On That Note: Jazz Elegics*
David Harsent – from *Marriage*
Michael Hofmann – *The Doppler Effect*
Glyn Maxwell – *The Paving Stones*
Paula Meehan – *Ectopic*
Grace Nichols – *Cosmic Disco*
Peter Reading – *In Marfa, TX*
Peter Redgrove – *Circus Wheel*
William Scammell – *Blue*
Ken Smith – *Near Barking*
Charles Tomlinson – *Ode to Memory*
Hugo Williams – *Slapstick*

Poems written in fireworks

Wendy Cope – *Fireworks Poems One and Two*
Tom Leonard – *Fireworks Poems, I, II, and III*
Christopher Reid – *Fire-bytes*
Kit Wright – *Fireworks Poems*

* Correct time of going to press. Precise placement of poems during the festival may have been slightly different.

Poem franked on letters

Carol Ann Duffy – –/–/99

Poems placed round Salisbury on everyday items: beer mats, bus tickets, billboards, carrier bags, etc.

Dannie Abse – *Gaiety at the Crematorium*
David Dabydeen – *Carnival Boy*
Amanda Dalton – *Tuesdays*
Maura Dooley – *Eclipse*
Lavinia Greenlaw – *The Spirit of the Staircase*
Andrew Greig – *A Night Rose*
Tobias Hill – *Later*
Mick Imlah – *1860*
Peter Porter – *Last Words*
Sheenagh Pugh – *Author, Author*
Deryn Rees Jones – *Plums*
Carol Rumens – *The Talk Pen*
Eva Salzman – *To the Enemy*
Pauline Stainer – *The Snake-dancer*

Poem flown from an aeroplane

Matthew Sweeney – *A Smell of Fish*

Poems projected on to public buildings

W. N. Herbert – *Lines on the West Face of Salisbury Cathedral* (on cathedral)
Selima Hill – *Arkansasoline* (on library)
Sean O'Brien – *Law* (on courthouse)

Poems by poets in residence during the festival

Paul Farley – *Fly* (residency with the army)
Sophie Hannah – *Long for this World* (residency at Spire Radio)
Roger McGough – *The Wrong Beds* (residency with the *Salisbury Journal*)
Katherine Pierpoint – *It Went By Very Fast* (residency with the police)
Neil Rollinson – *Helpline* (residency on the internet)

Poems by poets involved in projects during the festival

Jackie Kay – *Smoking Under Stars* (judging schools poetry competition)
Jamie McKendrick – *Good Hedges* (writing poem for film made with Rupert Jones, film-maker)
Adrian Mitchell – *Orpheus with the Beasts and Birds* (running workshops with origami artist, Dave Brill)
Edwin Morgan – *The Demon Judges a Father* (writing for a cathedral service)

Poems displayed in shop windows

Fleur Adcock – *A Visiting Angel* (children's clothes shop)
Fred D'Aguiar – *Foot Print* (shoe shop)
Peter Armstrong – *The Dean Surveys the Lingerie
    Dept.* (department store)
Sujata Bhatt – *One of Those Days* (aromatherapy shop)
Charles Boyle – *Casual Work* (station hotel)
Alan Brownjohn – *Grain* (grocery shop)
Kate Clanchy – *Feller, Son and Daughter* (butcher)
David Constantine – *School Parties in the Museum* (museum)
John Glenday – *Genesis* (cathedral shop)
Tracy Herd – *Black Swan* (ballet shop)
Alan Jenkins – *Her Last Nightdress* (launderette)
Mimi Khalvati – *The Fabergé Egg* (jeweller)
Roddy Lumsden – *Makeover* (hairdresser)
Sarah Maguire – *The Florist's at Midnight* (florist's)
Blake Morrison – *Against Dieting* (burger bar)
Bernard O'Donoghue – *Philomela* (wool and knitting shop)
Ruth Padel – *Hey Sugar, Take a Walk on the Wild
    Side* (deli)
Maurice Riordan – *The Cook's Night Out* (kitchen shop)
Robin Robertson – *Wedding the Locksmith's
    Daughter* (locksmith)
Anne Rouse – *To the Unknown Lover* (bicycle shop)
Peter Sansom – *Chippie* (chip shop)
Penelope Shuttle – *Scholar's Shop* (second-hand shop)
Anne Stevenson – *A Ballad for Apothecaries* (chemist)
George Szirtes – *Flash* (photography shop)
Susan Wicks – *Optician* (optician)

John Hartley Williams – *How the First Kite was Flown* (kite shop)

Gerard Woodward – *Giant* (dolls' house shop)

Poems read within a new composition by Gordon McPherson premiered at the festival

Simon Armitage – *The Way*

John Burnside – *Two Salisbury Sonnets*

Peter Didsbury – *Not the Noise of the World*

Douglas Dunn – *Dinner*

Vicki Feaver – *Speech*

Medbh McGuckian – *Our Lady's Bedstraw*

Edwin Morgan – *The Demon Judges a Father*

Tom Paulin – *Sarum's Pride*

Poems carved or written on stone, wood and glass, etc., in and around the Cathedral

Charles Causley – *In Asciano*

Robert Crawford – *Mite*

Kathleen Jamie – *Hoard*

Michael Longley – *The Beech Tree*

Paul Muldoon – *The Breather*

Eiléan Ní Chuilleanáin – *To the Angel in the Stone*

Tom Paulin – *Sarum's Prize*

Poems tattooed on the body of a volunteer

Michael Donaghy – *Tattoos*

Poems displayed on the Ladies and Gents at the Salisbury Arts Centre

Ian Duhig – *American Graffiti: I. Women's Room, II. Men's Room*

Index of Titles